THE BALANCING ACT

Also in the Women in Academe series:

Women and Academic Leadership:
Professional Strategies, Personal Choices

Most College Students Are Women:
Implications for Teaching, Learning, and Policy

THE BALANCING ACT

Gendered Perspectives in Faculty Roles and Work Lives

Edited by

Susan J. Bracken, Jeanie K. Allen,
and Diane R. Dean

Foreword by Ann E. Austin

Sty/us

STERLING, VIRGINIA

Copyright © 2006 by Stylus Publishing, LLC.

Published by Stylus Publishing, LLC
22883 Quicksilver Drive
Sterling, Virginia 20166-2102

Library of Congress Cataloging-in-Publication-Data
    The balancing act : gendered perspectives in faculty roles and work lives / edited by Susan J. Bracken, Jeanie K. Allen and Diane R. Dean ; Foreword by Ann E. Austin.
        p.   cm.— (Women in academe series)
    Includes bibliographical references and index.
    ISBN 1-57922-148-3 (hardcover : alk. paper)—
    ISBN 1-57922-149-1 (pbk. : alk. paper)
        1. Women college teachers—United States.   2. Women college teachers—Recruiting—United States.   3. Universities and colleges—United States—Faculty.   I. Bracken, Susan J., 1964–   II. Allen, Jeanie K., 1951–   III. Dean, Diane R., 1967–   IV. Series.
        LB2332.32.B35   2006
        378.1'2082—dc22   2005026728

ISBN: 1-57922-148-3 (cloth) / 13-digit ISBN: 978-1-57922-148-5

ISBN: 1-57922-149-1 (paper) / 13-digit ISBN: 978-1-57922-149-2

Printed in the United States of America

All first editions printed on acid free paper that meets the American National Standards Institute Z39-48 Standard.

Bulk Purchases

Quantity discounts are available for use in workshops and for staff development.
Call 1-800-232-0223

First Edition, 2006

10   9   8   7   6   5   4   3   2   1

CONTENTS

ACKNOWLEDGMENTS

This project would not have been possible without the hard work and support of many people who believe in the vision of balanced work lives for college and university faculty. We sincerely appreciate everything you have done! We especially wish to thank John von Knorring, Judy Coughlin, Karen Haley, Mary Dee Wenniger, and, of course, all the contributing authors.

Sue Bracken

Thank you to my family—Jeff, Trish, Laura—and also to Trish, Jay, Erica, and Evan for their love and support. And a thank you to my former and current colleagues whose presence in my work life has made a positive, lasting impact. You are terrific.

Jeanie Allen

I would like to thank my husband, Charlie, for his constant encouragement. Special thanks, also, to my mother, Ann Kattan, for cheering me on throughout my life. In addition, I want to recognize and thank all of the women I have had the privilege of meeting through the Women's Caucus of the American Association of Higher Education, as well as all of the women who have been colleagues, friends, and mentors in my life.

Diane Dean

I would like to thank my husband, John Giglio, for his support and encouragement. Thank you, also, to Norma Burgess, Katie Embree, Joseph Hankin, Arthur Levine, Sharon McDade, Elizabeth Miller, and the many members of the Women's Caucus of the American Association for Higher Education, whose friendship and mentoring I value greatly. This volume grew out of our collective mission and vision for equity in academe.

FOREWORD

Ann E. Austin

Today in the early part of the twenty-first century, American higher education institutions continue to hold a highly significant place in the national and international landscape. Universities and colleges serve society through the research produced, the students taught, the community issues addressed, and the ideas examined, challenged, and expanded. The faculty members in each university and college are the key resource ensuring that the work of higher education institutions occurs at a high level of quality and excellence. For many years, the notion of the professoriate brought up images of full-time, tenured or tenure-stream faculty members, most typically male and white. But the ranks of faculty members are changing rapidly. Many universities and colleges are appointing faculty into part-time and non-tenure-stream positions. Many institutions also are committed to diversifying the faculty ranks to include more women and scholars of color. Additionally, the nature of faculty work is changing, as universities and colleges welcome more diverse students; engage in a wide array of activities to serve their communities; respond to various expectations from employers, parents, legislators, and others; and adopt technology to aid and expand their impact.

This book addresses the broad topic of the changing nature of faculty roles and work lives, and more specifically focuses on the challenges confronted by—and the strategies used by—women and men faculty members as they manage their professional roles and personal lives. As part of a book series on "Women in Academe," this first volume concerns work/family issues for men and women faculty as well as gendered aspects of the academy. In particular, it offers views of faculty lives and work that expand readers' understanding of who the current faculty are and the kinds of issues that many faculty members confront each day as they strive to fulfill multiple responsibilities at work and at home. Additionally, it suggests institutional policies that may more fully support the diverse faculty members working in universities and colleges today.

In this foreword, I take up several issues. First, I answer the question of why readers, institutional leaders, and faculty members themselves should care about the academic workplace and how faculty members experience their work lives. Second, I highlight key themes that weave through the chapters of this book, all of which concern the nature of the academic workplace and how faculty members manage their responsibilities. Third, I explore various implications of the issues and themes highlighted in this work. What steps and strategies might institutional leaders and academic colleagues consider at their own institutions to enhance the quality of the academic workplace? What institutional policies and practices would support more fully the diverse group of faculty members who are carrying out the important work American universities and colleges are committed to?

Why Academic Work Life Issues Are Important

Discussion of the academic workplace tends to bring out a range of opinions. Some observers, often those not directly familiar with work within a college or university, comment that the academic workplace looks very appealing and far less demanding than the business world or other sectors. Such observers cite as evidence that faculty members typically meet classes only between six and fifteen hours a week, and have great autonomy as to how they spend the rest of their time. They note that many faculty members can arrange their own schedules, come and go as they like, and seem to have little direct supervision. Faculty members themselves are usually quick to point out that meeting classes is the tip of the iceberg, since, for example, good teaching requires extensive preparation, time out of class with individual students or small groups, and serious attention to assessment, grading, and feedback. Furthermore, most faculty members have other responsibilities, which, depending on the individual's appointment, can include research and publication, student advising, institutional committee work and leadership duties, development of new curricula, interactions and ongoing work with groups within the community, involvement in scholarly and professional associations, guidance and mentoring of new faculty members and graduate students, and attention to maintaining records and work-related materials.

Other observers, often individuals within the academy who have been in faculty rank for a number of years, observe that the nature and organization of faculty work, particularly in institutions with tenure systems, has worked well for many years. These individuals often love their work, take it very seriously, and are highly conscientious in fulfilling a multitude of tasks. They deeply appreciate the autonomy and flexibility that faculty members have come to enjoy, particularly at major research universities, and they understand and uphold the responsibility that the academy and individual faculty members have to society for the privilege of engaging in faculty work. For these individuals, concerns expressed by other faculty members about the nature of faculty work and the challenges of managing multiple responsibilities can appear ungrateful, cynical, and even ridiculous. These faculty members may wonder whether newer faculty are unwilling to work hard, not enough committed to their work, or simply prone to complaining.

Recognizing that discussion of the academic workplace can elicit these kinds of concerns from observers external and internal to universities or colleges, I offer several reasons why institutional leaders and faculty members should consider seriously the nature of the academic workplace and the challenges confronting many faculty members today. Interest in the academic workplace is not new (Austin & Gamson, 1983); but attention to the nature of the academic workplace is especially important today. The core of my argument is that attention to the quality of the workplace and to institutional strategies and policies for supporting a diverse array of faculty members to manage the demands in their lives will enrich the quality of work in universities and colleges. Such attention does not diminish the expectation that faculty members must be committed, serious, and engaged, but rather provides an environment in which all members of the faculty can contribute optimally to the critically important missions of universities and colleges. Such attention to the quality of the academic workplace also recognizes that the twenty-first-century university and college includes a diverse group of faculty members—women and men in a range of appointment types—with an array of circumstances, needs, and interests. And furthermore, the involvement of such a diverse group of faculty members is essential to institutional excellence.

What are the reasons that the quality of the workplace should be an institutional concern? First, as significant retirement rates are projected in the coming decade, universities and colleges will need to hire extensive replacements. And, since the proportion of women completing academic degrees is increasing (National Center for Education Statistics, 2001, 2003), many of the most well-trained and promising young scholars that universities and colleges may wish to recruit for open faculty positions will be women.

Furthermore, increasing the ranks of female faculty, as well as increasing the number of faculty of color (women and men), are important goals at many universities and colleges. As student bodies become more diverse, students need to see role models among the faculty with characteristics similar to their own. Thus, universities and colleges want to attract and retain a diverse faculty.

However, aspects of faculty work are not as promising for women as for men. Although women have been entering the faculty ranks for some time, inequities still are common in the experiences of male and female faculty members. Overall, salary patterns and promotion patterns are not yet equitable. And, as chapters in this book point out, family responsibilities can present challenging circumstances for women faculty. The chapter by Mason, Goulden, and Wolfinger shows that women with children are less likely than men to be appointed to tenure-stream positions in the first years out of graduate school. In the long term, women faculty are more likely than male colleagues to delay childbearing until their late 30s and they are twice as likely to indicate they have had fewer children than they would have liked. In their chapter, Wolf-Wendel and Ward explain that pregnant women, often new to their positions, sometimes must find their own temporary replacements for the class periods they will miss to give birth, and women with babies often grapple with an inhospitable environment for handling some of their parental responsibilities.

Offering an academic workplace that enables women candidates to envision the possibilities of including both professional and family dimensions in their lives is likely to be an important part of attractive recruitment packages. Equally important for retention of a diverse faculty body will be for institutions to provide environments that support women faculty as they simultaneously build excellent careers and meet their personal responsibilities.

Interest in family-friendly work environments is not only a women's issue, however. An earlier study sponsored by the American Association for Higher Education titled *Heeding New Voices* reported that, among aspiring and early-career scholars, both men and women hope to create careers that enable them to find "balance" and flexibility in their personal and professional lives (Rice, Sorcinelli, & Austin, 2000). Men and women scholars seek environments where they can manage effectively both personal and professional responsibilities. While childbirth obviously has a direct physical impact on women, men in their 20s and 30s often want and expect to participate actively in child rearing and family life, particularly given changes in gender roles in recent decades in American society. Thus, institutional policies that recognize personal needs, such as arrangements for spousal hires and family leave options, are attractive to many early-career faculty members.

Additionally, some doctoral students considering faculty careers are concerned about the overly hectic pace of life that they observe among their faculty members (Austin, 2002; Nyquist et al., 1999). Some of these potential faculty members are musing over whether an academic career will truly offer them the kind of work environment in which they can pursue their scholarly passions and the kind of life in which they can find both personal and professional meaning. Furthermore, some early-career faculty are reconsidering a professorial career (Rice et al., 2000). Such musings are important if they affect the likelihood of talented young scholars choosing to enter or remain in academe. Interest in the quality of the academic work life becomes not only a personal issue, but also an institutional one.

In addition to enhancing the interest of early-career faculty in entering and pursuing careers in academe, institutional attention to the quality of the academic workplace has implications for scholarly productivity. Faculty members who know that family needs, such as child care, are adequately addressed can turn their attention more fully to professional matters. Institutions that provide arrangements for short-term care for sick children, for example, enable faculty who are parents to manage teaching responsibilities even when faced with sudden illness in the family. The Creamer chapter in this volume argues that institutional efforts to remove barriers that inhibit or limit collaboration among faculty couples could enhance scholarly productivity. The Hart chapter details a case study of an institution that attempts meaningful change.

Many organizations already offer policies that help employees manage and balance the various responsibilities in their lives. As prominent members of their communities, higher education institutions can join other organizations in providing examples of how to construct workplaces that meet organizational goals while also recognizing human needs of organization members. Finding ways to help talented people achieve success and fulfillment in both their professional and personal lives is a challenging but worthy goal for an advanced society. Engaging in efforts to try out and assess the impact of various policies is another way in which higher education institutions can contribute to the overall betterment of the broader society.

For all the reasons discussed here, higher education institutions should consider the nature and quality of the academic workplace and particularly the ways in which universities and colleges support faculty members in managing professional and personal roles. The issue should not be interpreted as an example of uncommitted individuals who are unwilling to engage in the sustained and often difficult work of being a scholar. Rather, efforts to create workplace environments that address the needs of many faculty members to handle professional and personal responsibilities will strengthen the excellence of American higher education. Faculty bodies will become more diverse. Individual faculty members, who in today's world represent a great array of personal circumstances and appointment types, will be supported as they commit themselves to doing their best work. And examples will be provided for the broader public of ways to create workplaces that achieve organizational goals while enabling individual employees to live fulfilling lives with multiple responsibilities. This book provides information, insights, and suggestions to further the conversation.

References

Austin, A. E. (2002, January/February). Preparing the next generation of faculty: Graduate education as socialization to the academic career. *Journal of Higher Education, 73*(2), 94–122.

Austin, A. E., & Gamson, Z. F. (1983). *The academic workplace: New demands, greater tensions.* ASHE-ERIC/Higher Education Research Report No. 10. Washington, DC: Association for the Study of Higher Education.

National Center for Education Statistics. (2001). *The integrated postsecondary education data system (IPEDS) salaries, tenure, and fringe benefits of full-time instructional faculty survey.* Washington, DC: Author.

National Center for Education Statistics. (2003). *The integrated postsecondary education data system (IPEDS) completions survey.* Washington, DC: Author.

Nyquist, J. D., Manning, L., Wulff, D. H., Austin, A. E., Sprague, J., Fraser, et al. (1999, May/June). On the road to becoming a professor: The graduate student experience. *Change,* 18–27.

Rice, R. E., Sorcinelli, M. D., & Austin, A. E. (2000). *Heeding new voices: Academic careers for a new generation.* Washington, DC: American Association of Higher Education.

INTRODUCTION:
THE PAST, PRESENT, AND FUTURE

Women's Studies, Higher Education, and Praxis

Susan J. Bracken, Jeanie K. Allen, and Diane R. Dean

This book features a collection of research studies about contemporary faculty roles and work lives in higher education. As coeditors, we began this project as an outgrowth of our involvement with the former *American Association for Higher Education's Women's Caucus*. Historically, the caucus dedicated its work to the professional development and advocacy for women in higher education. Our goals as recent leaders of the caucus were to create opportunities to increase the visibility of gendered research that influences women's work lives within the academy and, subsequently, to stimulate interest and collective action in improving faculty work lives for women and men. Together, our respective areas of scholarship include women's studies, adult education, interdisciplinary studies, and higher education.

As coeditors, we have had many opportunities during the past three years to share with each other our professional pathways, our personal stories, and our academic interests. We quickly learned that we all share an appreciation for the importance of praxis and the contribution of women's studies as a presence in the academy. In each of our own academic careers, women's studies has played a strong foundational role in shaping our scholarship and professional pathways. It was this series of conversations that prompted us to include a women's studies focus as part of our own reflections in this work.

Therefore, we will briefly revisit the historical development of women's studies in American higher education, and its influence on the scholarship featured in this volume. Honoring the contributions of those who came before us and understanding the stories, strategies, policies, and issues are not merely tributes to the past, but they offer an opportunity to substantively reflect and to develop frameworks for understanding current efforts to improve the nature of faculty roles and work lives. From that foundation, we will then present a brief outline of what we believe continued interdisciplinary study and strategic praxis can do to further the research and practical application of the scholarship of the contributing authors and of others who are interested in understanding and improving the holistic and equitable quality of faculty work lives.

Fleeting Shadows of the Past: Women's Studies and the Institution of Higher Education

Many of us associate the late 1960s with dramatic social change in the United States—the civil rights movement, the Vietnam War, and the women's movement were debated and visible in all aspects of societal life. This period of flux and angst was also reflected within higher education. Life on campuses was markedly different than it is now, with differential gender rules for administrative life, student residence halls, social climate, academic expectations, and areas of study. Very few women were entering the academy as faculty members (12% of doctoral degrees awarded in 1966 were to women compared to 51% in 2001), and those who were either graduate students or new faculty were experiencing campuses that were not sensitive to gender issues of access, pay equity, sexual harassment, campus safety, or diverse academic content.

It was within this context that women's groups formed on campuses across the United States in order to deal with climate issues—paralleling the women's consciousness-raising groups forming in communities. In addition to self-discovery and growth in understanding gender roles in society, the campus women's groups lobbied for fair treatment; improved women's health, safety, and other services; entrance to disciplines that were essentially inaccessible to women; resolution of hiring and promotion issues; and more. Participants primarily focused on understanding how women's social identities were shaping their lives and the lives of others and, in turn, how this knowledge and understanding connected to higher education policies and practices. Marilyn Boxer (1998) describes the reaction of male faculty members to the rapidly changing landscape:

> Getman's candid account neatly complements Hochschild's 1973 essay, for he relates how women's new aspirations to academic careers affected marital relationships and departmental manners. Recalling a dinner party at a Midwestern university in 1969, Getman quotes a chemistry professor as commenting "during dessert" that the "women's movement is going to destroy scholarship in America. We're a perfect example. I am on the verge of a major conceptual breakthrough that I could achieve soon if only Ginny wouldn't keep insisting that I look after the children all the time." Another guest, a professor of English, lamented that he thought that his wife wanted him "to stop working on my novel so that she can get her B.A." Getman now realizes that the comfortable male-dominated world in which we dwelt was soon to become a thing of the past. (p. 235)

Joan Williams (1999) theorizes that a number of the structural problems with contemporary faculty roles stem from this traditional and masculine vision of academic faculty life designed around the notion of a male faculty member with an available full-time stay-at-home spouse supporting his work. She suggests that real change will result when we begin to design faculty roles that take into account the realities of modern society.

In 1969, the first women's studies program in the United States opened its doors at San Diego State University, followed the next year by Cornell University in 1970. They offered beginning courses on general women's issues, and served as the primary voice and advocacy group for women in higher education. Initially, there was doubt as to the staying power of women's studies—some thought it was a fad that would come and go, particularly in terms of intellectual theoretical development as an academic discipline (*Women's Studies*, 1970). Berkeley commissioned a senate study examining the status of women. The findings were not surprising: only 15 women on the entire campus had the rank of full professor; faculty, administrators, current and former graduate students reported numerous, serious inequities such as "rules which prevented wives with Ph.D.s from being hired at the same campus where their husbands worked, reluctance to tenure qualified women or promote them through academic ranks; preference awarded to men in graduate admissions, and after admission, in financial and intellectual support; crediting male colleagues for research and research reports written by women . . . substantial psychological abuse at all levels of academic hierarchy" (Gerrard, 2002, p. 66).

When I joined a women's studies program as an advisor in the early 1990s, there was less doubt about women's studies' intellectual veracity or staying power, but most programs were still consumed with the slow, formative process of building organizational stability, resources, curriculum, and campus visibility. Then, as in many programs or departments now, many of the courses were taught by faculty in other disciplinary departments, as cross-listed courses or voluntary teaching overloads. As a result of the academic and internal organizational focus, the campus advocacy roles were difficult to pursue with equal energy. Marilyn Boxer (1998) discusses the evolution of women's studies programs in her book, *When Women Ask the Questions: Creating Women's Studies in America.* She explains that, very quickly, women's studies shifted not only to serve a women's activist and advocacy role on campus but also to an intellectual role. It began with systematic questioning of the academic content across disciplines. Did it include women's voices? Were women's perspectives considered a legitimate part of research and teaching? Why or why not? What could existing disciplinary work look like, when shaped by feminist perspectives? This now 35-year shift in scholarship across the disciplines offers a platform that enables contemporary scholars and students to bring subjectivity, feminist method, and research topics, previously considered to be in the private domain or outside of legitimate scholarship, to the forefront in the academy.

By the 1990s, there were more than 600 women's studies programs (Boxer, 1998), and that number has continued to grow each year. It's hard now to imagine the absence of contemporary critical and feminist theory, feminist methodology, the inclusion of gendered research questions, and the increased presence of women on college campuses. Women's studies has changed curriculums, classroom pedagogical approaches, the nature of research methodology, offered feminist theoretical frameworks, and continues to maintain an advocacy presence. There have been moments during our academic careers when many of us have had to make difficult choices weighted against perceived professional risk (in connection to gender); it is with this in mind we cannot understate the past contributions of the scholar-activists who challenged or worked diligently to improve the higher education system.

At this point, some women's studies scholars who are reading this essay are probably anxious to interject "Have we *really* made that much progress?" Many scholars legitimately argue that we are slow to advance and that in "virtually every field and subfield, in almost every cohort and at almost every point in their teaching and research careers, women [still] advance more slowly and earn less money than men. The history of the profession in the past few decades suggests that the problem of women's lower status in academe will not dissipate in the fullness of time" (Pratt, 2002, p. 13). The research findings in this book certainly point to sustained and systemic equity and climate issues in the academy.

While it would be foolish to argue that gender equity in the academy has fully arrived, the intent of this essay is to purposefully interject the presence of women's studies into the discourse on faculty work lives in the academy. Women's studies has directly and indirectly created a literal and figurative space for this type of scholarship to take place. Whether that scholarship relies directly upon feminist theoretical constructs and/or indirectly relies upon the created space to openly research and discuss issues of balancing work and family lives in academics, women's studies has made a contribution that many contemporary scholars in other disciplines may be unaware of.

In the past, activism and political involvement were so intertwined with academic women's studies that they were discussed and conceptually viewed together. Women's studies scholars were overtly political and committed to activism within and outside of the academy. Currently, it is difficult to make that blanket assumption. There is a broader range of accepted women's, women's studies, feminist, and activist scholarship. To some scholars and students, women's studies is *scholarship about, for, and by women*. It places gendered perspectives and women's lived experience at the center of scholarly inquiry, but does not necessarily explicitly include acts of praxis or action. Some feminist scholars define the dissemination of their intellectual scholarship as activist acts in and of themselves, and look to others to pick up that scholarship and advocate for social change.

Contemporary scholar-activists in women's studies seek to study, describe, and explain the root cause(s) of women's oppression in society and identification as a women's studies scholar includes dedication to the core principle of *praxis,* the integration of theory and practice. Women's studies scholar-activists seek to collectively research, craft solutions, and advocate for actions that improve women's lives and more social equity in society.

Connecting Constructs of Feminist Praxis to Research on Faculty Roles and Worklives

The scholarship featured in this book was selected because of its connection to the topic of gendered faculty roles and work lives in higher education, and because of our belief that it is essential to view these issues collectively in addition to their dissemination as independent pieces of research. We know from the chapter by Mary Ann Mason, Marc Goulden, and Nicholas H. Wolfinger that we still face serious pipeline issues—women and men are not entering academic careers at a rate proportional to their degree attainment, and when they do enter academia, women are dropping off in terms of tenure-track positions, achieving tenure or promotion, or in establishing family and personal lives while pursuing tenure. Once women and men are in tenure-track positions, Lisa Wolf-Wendel and Kelly Ward help us to understand the nature of the experience of women faculty trying to concurrently establish families and careers. They affirm what many of us may have observed in our own institutions and lives: that many women are unaware of institutional parental leave policies, and even with that awareness, may be hesitant to access or utilize those policies. Women in their study described informal understandings of expectations to have only one baby while tenure track or of trying to precisely time pregnancies for May due dates that don't interfere with academic schedules. Carol Colbeck's study is unique and extremely valuable in helping us to challenge assumptions and ask new questions about how men and women integrate their work and maintain personal/professional boundaries. One important concept we can draw from her work is that one size does not fit all and we need to purposefully allow room for colleagues to creatively and collaboratively develop solutions and openly support each other in learning strategies that maintain productive work lives *and* satisfying personal lives. Elizabeth Creamer's research and scholarship on dual-career couples is critical in helping us to think through the issues academic couples must navigate in balancing their work and family lives, as well as the gendered constructions that influence others' perceptions of their partnerships. Anna Neumann, Aimee LaPointe Terosky, and Julie Schell help us to re-conceptualize and understand posttenure faculty as agents of their own learning and careers. We don't often think about mid-career experiences or how faculty members experience the posttenure transition, and their work reminds us that we do have agency and can share strategies and further develop agency at all points of our careers. And finally, Jeni Hart presents case study data on a campus attempting to define and develop strategies for dealing with women's issues.

In compiling this book we hope that the range of scholarship presented and the collective presence adds a sense of cumulative value and power to the work that lies ahead. We have chosen to present a basic historical frame from which to understand and appreciate the role of women's studies and feminist scholarship and to affirm the value of praxis in higher education. As tempting as it is to write a chapter that synthesizes the complex feminist theoretical perspectives, which add insight and inform the issues, we believe that we can accomplish our own goals of feminist scholarship by synthesizing important current research on issues in the academy and by framing it within the context of women's studies.

We would also like to suggest concrete next steps for those of you who would like to take tangible steps within your own work environments to effect change for the better.

These suggestions include the following:

1. *Maintain vigilant awareness of campus work lives and environments by designing gender research that questions "what we define and accept as normal."* When we become comfortable with the status quo, it is challenging at best to step back and appropriately reframe questions. In addition to asking how women are navigating inequities within the higher education system, we can also ask ourselves why we are all participating in shaping imbalanced or inequitable workplace practices and what we can actively do to make changes.

2. *Embrace "the personal is political" in your work and look for it in the work of others.* In terms of equitable, healthy work environments, what is viewed and framed as good for women is also good for all members of the campus community *and* essential for the longevity of the academy. We can and should be critically reflective of our own and others' participation, leadership, and agency in creating positive and equitable work environments.

3. *Re-envision yourselves as adult learners in addition to experts in your respective fields.* Most faculty are accustomed to operating in a professional system that casts them as individualistic research experts and highly specialized teachers. In fact, all of us are also lifelong adult

learners in need of ongoing personal and professional opportunities to grow and to learn. Faculty and other campus community members should expect and solicit regular professional development opportunities, not only in our content expertise and supporting technology areas, but in how to create and contribute to healthy, creative, and collaborative work environments. Systematic institutional change will require policy changes at all levels in addition to renewed dedication to education, learning, and personal reflection.

4. *Seek to identify problems and gaps balanced with appreciative inquiry that uncovers noteworthy positive structures and practices.* Most researchers work to identify a gap or a problem, and then to solve it. When engaged in problem solving complex sociological issues that influence our own lives, it is easy to focus exclusively on what we are not doing well and on identifying and labeling problems. It is equally tempting to view solutions as lying outside of ourselves and residing in actions others should take instead. We need to take ownership of our own actions, drawing upon what we learn from those who already successfully innovate, collaborate, and work toward more meaningful and equitable faculty work lives.

References

Boxer, M. J. (1998). *When women ask the questions: Creating women's studies in America.* Baltimore: John Hopkins University Press.

Gerrard, L. (2002). Berkeley, 1969: A memoir. *Women's Studies Quarterly: Then and Now. 30*(3&4), 60–72.

Griffith, S. C. (2002). Using women's studies to change the university for all women: Report from the University of Wisconsin-Superior. *Women's Studies Quarterly: Then and Now. 30*(3&4), 90–98.

Pratt, A. V. (2002). Then and now in women's studies: My pedagogical request. *Women's Studies Quarterly: Then and Now, 30*(3&4), 12–26.

Williams, J. (1999). *Unbending gender: Why family and work conflict and what to do about it.* New York: Oxford University Press.

Women's studies. (1970, October 26). *Newsweek,* p. 61.

I

BABIES MATTER

Pushing the Gender Equity Revolution Forward

Mary Ann Mason, Marc Goulden, and Nicholas H. Wolfinger

In the last three decades, women have made impressive strides toward equity in the academy. From a relatively small, marginalized population in the early 1970s, women now seem poised to become the future heirs of the ivory tower. Women already make up 59% of master's, 57% of bachelor's degree recipients, and half of all U.S. Ph.D.s granted to American citizens (see Figure 1.1; National Center for Education Statistics [NCES], 2003a; National Science Foundation [NSF], 2004c). Despite these impressive gains, women represent only 26% of the associate and full professors in the United States (NCES, 2003b), and there remains a barrier to the achievement of full gender equity: the failure of the academy to welcome women with families, particularly women with babies, into the fold.

The observation that women Ph.D.s might be leaking out the tenure-track pipeline at disproportionately higher rates than men and encountering barriers in their pursuit of tenure led us to our current research effort, the "Do Babies Matter?" project.[1] Using data from the Survey of Doctorate Recipients (SDR) (NSF 2004b) and the University of California Faculty Work and Family survey (Mason, Stacy, & Goulden, 2003), we examined several related issues—the effects of family formation on career progression, the effects of having a faculty career on family patterns, and the nature of work/family conflict for academic parents. These analyses (Mason & Goulden, 2002, 2004a, 2004b; Wolfinger, Mason, & Goulden, 2004) have positioned us to propose specific improvements to existing family accommodation

FIGURE 1.1
Ph.D. recipients from U.S. universities by ethnicity/gender
(U.S citizens only), 1973–2003.

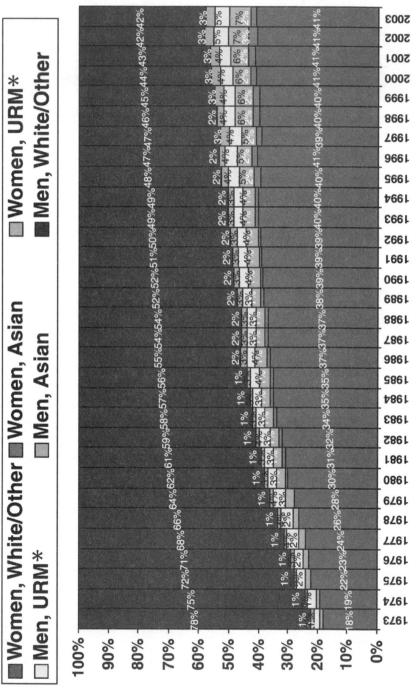

*Underrepresented minorities (URM) include African Americans, Hispanic Americans, and Native Americans.

policies, as well as to advocate for a family-friendly package of additional policies, resources, and services in the academy.

Problems in the Pipeline: Assessing Family Formation Effects on the Tenure Rates of Men and Women Ph.D.s

The SDR—a longitudinal, biennial, nationally representative survey of Ph.D.s' postdegree employment status—has included family-related questions since 1981 (Clark, 1994; NSF, 1995, 2004b). It is an ideal data source for measuring the effects of gender and family on men and women's academic career progress. Although the SDR has been conducted for more than 30 years and includes more than 160,000 respondents, most well-known scholarly studies on faculty rank advancement and academic productivity have used other data sources (Cole & Zuckerman, 1987; Jacobs, 1996; Long, Allison, & McGinnis, 1993; Perna, 2001; Toutkoushian, 1999; Valian, 1998; Xie & Shauman, 1998). Only recently have scholars turned their attention to the SDR as a significant resource for investigating these types of issues (Ginther, 2001; Kulis, Sicotte, & Collins, 2002; Long, 2001; Mason & Goulden, 2002; NSF, 2004a).

Using SDR data (and controlling for broad disciplinary field, age at Ph.D. receipt, prestige of Ph.D. program, time-to-Ph.D. degree, calendar year of Ph.D., and ethnicity), we conducted two separate multivariate assessments: the effect of gender and family formation on the year-to-year likelihood of (1) men and women Ph.D.s entering a tenure-track position after Ph.D. receipt and (2) tenure-track men and women achieving tenure (Wolfinger et al., 2004).[2] These two analyses show that marriage and young children have a strong, negative effect on the probability of women *entering* tenure-track positions, but family status has no clear independent effect on determining whether tenure-track faculty eventually achieve tenure. Rather, all tenure-track women are less likely to eventually achieve tenure than tenure-track men.

Our findings illuminate the extent of problems in the tenure pipeline for women, particularly ones with family-related origins.[3] Figure 1.2 shows the year-by-year predicted probabilities of different gender-family groups entering a tenure-track position. In the first year out from the Ph.D., the high-water mark of tenure-track job entry, 16% of married men with children under 6 and 16% of single women without children under 6 are expected to

FIGURE 1.2
Securing a tenure track position after the Ph.D.

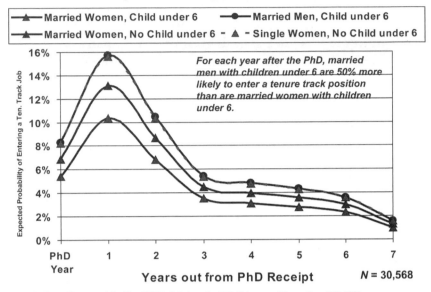

Source: Wolfinger, Mason, and Goulden (2004). Data from the SDR, Science and Humanities, 1981-1995.

enter a tenure-track position. In contrast, only 13% of married women without children under 6 and a paltry 10% of married women with children under 6 are predicted to do so. Thus, married men with children under 6 are 50% more likely than married women with children under 6 to join the ranks of tenure-track faculty in the first year out from the Ph.D.; this increased likelihood holds steady for all years after Ph.D. receipt. Because single women without children under 6 do as well as married men with children under 6, family formation completely explains why women are overall less likely than men to enter tenure-track positions (Wolfinger et al., 2004). The message is clear: for women, babies and marriage, particularly in combination, dramatically decrease their likelihood of entering a tenure-track faculty position.

Once women begin tenure-track jobs, family formation no longer explains their decreased likelihood of moving through the pipeline to tenure. Rather, as seen in Figure 1.3, tenure-track women, regardless of family status, are less likely than men to get tenure (Wolfinger et al., 2004). On a year-to-year basis, men are 20% more likely to achieve tenure than are women. We

FIGURE 1.3
Leaks in the pipeline: Tenure track to tenure.

For each year after securing a tenure track position, men are 20% more likely to achieve tenure than are women

Years out from Tenure Track Start Date   *N* = 10,845

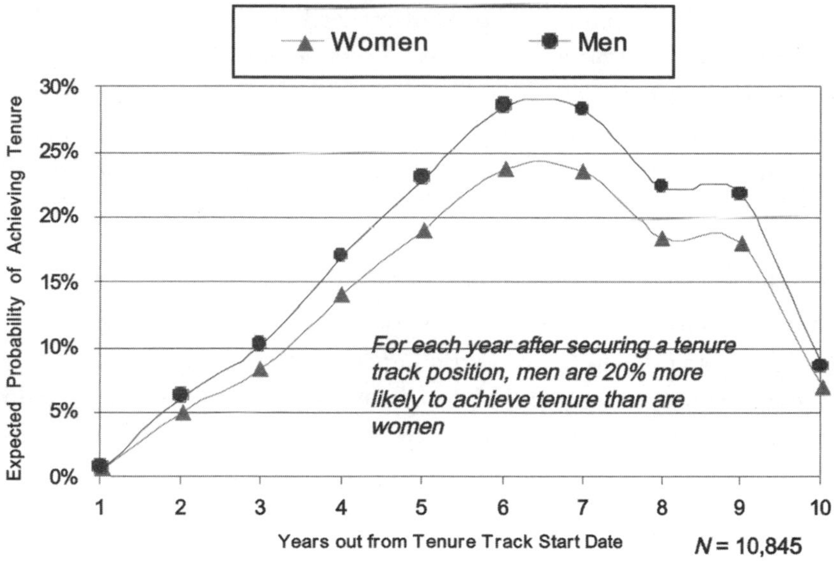

Source: Wolfinger, Mason and Goulden (2004). Data from the SDR, Science and Humanities, 1981-1995.

do not know why this is the case but suspect that factors such as discrimination may be at work (e.g., Valian, 1998; Williams, 2000).

This second leak for women, the tenure-track-to-tenure leak, is troubling, but the first leak is even more worrisome because it is earlier in the pipeline and thus has a compounding effect. Achieving tenure is obviously predicated on entering a tenure-track faculty position; thus married women, particularly those with young children, are lost to the professoriate within the first few years after Ph.D. receipt. As seen in Figure 1.2, the likelihood of entering a tenure-track position three or more years after receipt of the Ph.D. is remote, and with each passing year becomes even less probable.

Focusing in greater detail on this first critical leak in the pipeline to academic success, data from the 1997 SDR Science Survey contribute additional insight on the effects of family on women Ph.D.s' pursuit of tenure-track careers. Specifically, among Ph.D.s (1990 to 1995) in the sciences and social sciences who report that their career goal when they began their Ph.D. program was to be a faculty member, married women with children under 6 are the most likely (72%) to indicate that family responsibilities affected their job search (see Figure 1.4). In contrast, married men with children under 6 are the most likely of these groups to identify "no suitable job" as limiting their job search. Almost two-thirds of married women, with and without children under 6 (66% and 64%, respectively), indicated that spousal careers had limited their job search; and more than half of married women, with and without children under 6, cited location issues, or a desire not to move, as a factor limiting their job search. Of the various factors affecting the job search of single women without children under 6, "no suitable job" was most commonly cited (49%).

The fact that married women Ph.D.s are more likely than their male counterparts to indicate that their spouse's career limited their search for a faculty position should come as little surprise. They, like other married professional women, are overwhelmingly partnered with spouses who have full-time jobs. Among respondents to the 1997 SDR Sciences and Social Sciences Survey, 84% of married women Ph.D.s with a faculty career goal reported having a spouse who worked full-time. In contrast, only 36% of the married

FIGURE 1.4
Factors limiting search for career path job (among 1990 to 1995 science and social science Ph.D.s with professorial career goal).

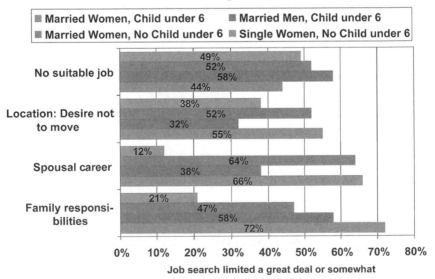

Source: Survey of Doctorate Recipients, Sciences, 1997.
Note: The use of NSF data does not imply NSF endorsement of research methods or conclusions contained in this report.

men with a faculty career goal indicated that their spouse worked full-time. Clearly women Ph.D.s are disproportionately affected by the need to take into account their spouse's careers.

Alone in the Ivory Tower: Family Outcomes Among Ladder-Rank Faculty and Second-Tier Women

This loss of women Ph.D.s with family responsibilities from tenure-track careers is only half the story. Using data from the SDR to answer the opposite question—what is the effect of tenure-track faculty careers on family formation?—we find that men and women have very different family formation patterns. Specifically, single women in tenure-track positions who are within three years of receiving their Ph.D.s are significantly less likely than single tenure-track men or single nontenure-track women to get married (37% lower probability than single tenure-track men and 34% lower probability than single nontenure-track faculty women). This pattern continues for 10 years after the first post-Ph.D. SDR interview, which we refer to as "first job." Conversely, tenure-track women who are married at first job are much more likely than tenure-track men and nontenure-track women to get divorced as their careers progress (37% greater risk of becoming divorced than married tenure-track men and 48% greater risk than married nontenure-track women).[4]

Tenure-track women are also less likely to have children at the beginning of their faculty career. After controlling for various professional and personal differences between respondents, tenure-track women are considerably less likely to have a child under 6 in the household at first job (17%) than are tenure-track men (38%), nontenure-track women (22%), and women Ph.D.s who are not employed (46%).[5]

Over time, these fertility differences, as measured by the presence of children under 6 in the household, only become more pronounced, with tenure-track women falling farther and farther behind. Figure 1.5 shows the likelihood for each two-year period after "first job" of each of these groups having a child under age 6 enter the household (if they do not already have a young child). Women Ph.D.s who are not employed show the highest rates of fertility, followed by tenure-track men, and nontenure-track women. Tenure-track women again have the lowest fertility rate. Figure 1.5 also demonstrates that all women Ph.D.s relative to men Ph.D.s experience a decline in fertility

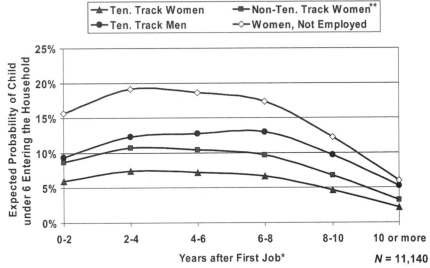

FIGURE 1.5

Having a child under age 6 enter the household after first job.*

*For individuals who had no child under 6 in household at first job, taken from first SDR survey, 0-4 years post-PhD.
**Non-Tenure Track, Part Time, or Not Working.
Source: SDR Science and Humanities Survey, 1981-1995. PhD recipients 1978-1994.

rates with each additional two-year period out from first job.[6] All told, women who begin their tenure-track career without children have less than one in three odds of ever having them. Twelve years out from Ph.D. receipt, a clear majority of tenure-track men (69%) are married with children, while only a minority of tenure-track women are married with children (41%; Mason & Goulden, 2004a, 2004b).

Differences in work status—part-time versus full-time—can partially explain career-track differences in the presence of children. As seen in Figure 1.6, full-time tenure-track and full-time nontenure-track women are the least likely to have a child under age 6 enter the household. Part-time employed women, tenure track or nontenure track, are considerably more fertile than full-time-employed women. Women Ph.D.s who are not working have the highest rate of fertility, but the part-time women are nearly as fertile.[7] The major trend here is clear: The less women Ph.D.s work, the more fertile they are. This suggests that the full-time nature of tenure-track faculty careers helps to explain why tenure-track women have such low fertility rates.

FIGURE 1.6

Women Ph.D.s: Having a child under age 6 enter the household after first job, by job type and full-time/part-time status.*

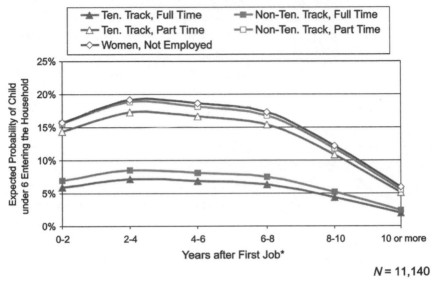

N = 11,140

*For individuals who had no child under 6 in household at first job, taken from first SDR survey, 0-4 years post-PhD.
Source: SDR Science and Humanities Survey, 1981-1995. PhD recipients 1978-1994.

Work, Family Life, and Faculty Recruitment and Retention

Why are women opting out, or being pushed out, of the academy? Why do men and women faculty have such different family formation patterns? The tension between work and family responsibilities—a tension that is experienced more strongly by women—is one answer to these questions. To better understand the significance of work and family issues in the lives of tenure-track faculty, and to test the effectiveness of existing family-friendly policies and resources, we designed and conducted the UC Work and Family Survey, which included all nine active University of California campuses. Of 8,705 faculty surveyed, 4,459 responded to the 14-page instrument (Mason et al., 2003), a 51% response rate. In their responses, thousands of UC tenure-track faculty men and women cite considerable difficulties in negotiating the competing demands of work and family.

These difficulties are especially pressing for women faculty ages 30 to 50 with children who report spending over 100 hours a week on professional, domestic, and caregiving activities (e.g., providing care for children, spouse, or elders). In contrast, men ages 30 to 50 with children, spend slightly over 85 hours a week, and all faculty ages 30 to 50 without children spend no more than 80 hours a week on these activities (Mason & Goulden, 2004a, 2004b). Thus, women with young children are particularly likely to experience what Hochschild (1997) has referred to as a time bind.

Even more telling are the average weekly caregiving hours of UC faculty by age at survey. As seen in Figure 1.7, women with children bear a disproportionate amount of the caregiving load in comparison to men with children, even though the overwhelming majority of both male and female UC faculty work full-time. It is not until around age 60 that the average number of weekly hours providing care to others comes close to converging for these different faculty groups. This suggests that family accommodation policies for faculty that focus only upon birth/adoption events fail to address the sizeable caregiving load that faculty parents, particularly mothers, continue to bear for up to two decades following a birth event.

Other data from the UC survey support the conclusion that work and

FIGURE 1.7
University of California faculty's average hours per week providing care, by gender, children, and age at survey.

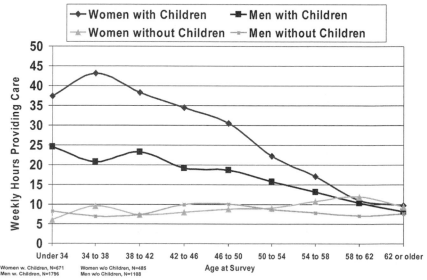

Source: Mason, Mary Ann, Angelica Stacy, and Marc Goulden. 2003. "The UC Faculty Work and Family Survey." (http://ucfamilyedge.berkeley.edu).

family tensions are common among UC faculty parents, particularly among women. Nearly half of women reported, for example, that certain career responsibilities—such as attending conferences or giving conference papers (46%), other professional work that requires travel away from home (48%), and the time-intensive activities of writing and publishing (48%)—cause them a great deal of stress in their parenting. In contrast, less than 30% of men faculty parents reported that the same activities placed a great deal of stress on their parenting (22% experienced a great deal of stress from attending conferences, 29% from writing and publishing, and 27% from doing fieldwork away from home) (Mason & Goulden, 2004b).

The UC data also reveal that many faculty attempt to minimize the negative consequences associated with parental obligations. As seen in Figure 1.8, substantial proportions of UC faculty parents, particularly mothers, avoid bringing their children to work because they worry that it would bother their colleagues; others tried to time childbirth in the summer; and still others missed important events in their children's lives because of professional demands or returned to work sooner than they would have liked after becom-

FIGURE 1.8
Work/family conflict among UC faculty parents.

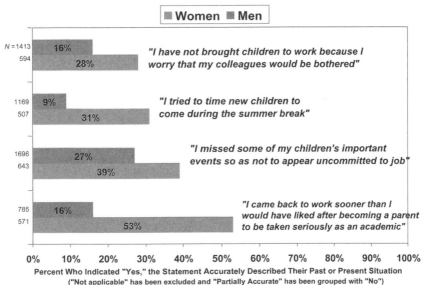

Source: Mason, Mary Ann, Angelica Stacy, and Marc Goulden. 2003. "The UC Faculty Work and Family Survey." (http://ucfamilyedge.berkeley.edu).

ing a parent to appear fully committed to their career.[8] These types of choices by parents demonstrate the complexity of conflicts related to parenting and academic careers.

Since 1988, the University of California-Berkeley (UCB), as part of the UC system, has had in place a series of progressive policies designed to level the playing field for faculty mothers and fathers. Nonetheless, we found that although UC's three cornerstone family accommodation policies—active service-modified duties (ASMD), tenure-clock extension, and paid leave—have existed for over a decade, too few faculty know about the policies and too few eligible faculty use them. Of all UC faculty respondents, only 50% knew about ASMD, which provides teaching relief for substantial caregivers around the time of a birth or adoption event; 66% knew about tenure-clock extension, which offers to substantial caregivers a one-year extension to the tenure clock per child/adoption event; 73% knew about paid leave for birth mothers, typically six weeks with possible extension for medical reasons; and only 38% knew about all three policies. Given the lack of awareness regarding these policies, it is not surprising to find that many eligible UC faculty did not use them. Among assistant professor women, only 45% used ASMD at their first eligible birth/adoption event, 30% used tenure-clock extension, and 52% used paid leave. The use rates for eligible assistant professor men were even lower, with only 7% using ASMD and 8% using tenure-clock extension (paid leave is only for birth mothers).

When eligible UC faculty were asked why they did not make use of the policies, two major issues came to the forefront: the aforementioned lack of knowledge, and fear of policy use. Specifically, 48% percent of ASMD-eligible women and 46% percent of ASMD-eligible men cited their lack of knowledge about the policy as a major reason for not using it. Perhaps of greater concern, 51% of eligible women and 26% of eligible men cited fear that it would hurt their careers as a major reason for not using ASMD.

Although a well-formulated publicity campaign could raise faculty's awareness of the policies, the fact that many eligible faculty forgo policy use because of fear points to more deeply rooted problems of institutional culture and climate. Echoing other findings (Drago & Williams, 2000; Williams, 2000), we found that many UC faculty avoided behavior that they feared might result in negative repercussions. This fear-based response was observable not only in the low use rates of existing family-friendly policies by eligible faculty, but also in the conscious attempts of faculty women to delay or forgo fertility (see also Armenti, 2004; Finkel & Olswang, 1996; Varner, 2000). Among UC faculty women, the most likely time to have a baby is 4–8 years out from the assistant professor hire date, around the time of tenure (Mason & Goulden, 2004a, 2004b), when the average age is 38–40 years old. In contrast, the most common time for men to have children is 0–4 years from the assistant professor hire date. Delaying or forgoing fertility is often not the desire of women faculty, as 40% of our faculty women (compared to just 20% of men) past the age of likely fertility, 40 to 60 years, indicated that they had fewer children than they wanted (Mason & Goulden, 2004a, 2004b).

Taken together, findings from the SDR and the UC survey show that gender equity in the academy has not yet been achieved. Although a higher proportion of women are receiving Ph.D.s than ever before, many are leaking out of the pipeline prior to procuring tenure-track academic jobs, and others are trading marriage and children in favor of success in the academy. For faculty women who choose to have both a tenure-track position and family, our findings highlight the immense challenges faced in terms of hours, stress, and work/family conflict. Making academic institutions family friendly goes beyond matters of gender equity; it is a necessary response to the growing number of women in higher education. Institutions that understand this fundamental change will enjoy a competitive advantage in recruitment and retention of faculty.

The UC Faculty Family Friendly Edge

Aided by a grant from the Alfred P. Sloan Foundation, we have been developing a comprehensive family-friendly package for UC ladder-rank faculty. This multiyear effort, known as the UC Faculty Family Friendly Edge (http://ucfamilyedge.berkeley.edu), seeks to strengthen existing policies and to supplement them with additional policies, resources, and services. Because no single policy or resource will be a panacea, a package of policies and resources is being developed to help faculty as their life and caregiving situations change over time.

Family Accommodation Policies

For academia to be fully equitable for men and women, the development of robust family accommodation policies for tenure-track faculty is essential. A series of revisions to the existing UC family accommodation polices are expected to be in place within the next half year.[9] One goal of the new policies is to make clear that ASMD and tenure-clock extension are entitlements. Previously, the policy language indicated that eligible faculty could request their use; now the language makes clear that these policies are part of business as usual and that eligible faculty should avail themselves of these accommodations. UC's Office of the President (UCOP) has requested that campuses provide central funds for the cost of replacement faculty when faculty take ASMD or paid leave. This removes the disincentive that some smaller departments had to provide these accommodations because of their expense. The policy revisions also provide birth mothers with an additional quarter or semester (depending on the campus's calendar type) of ASMD as a childbirth disability allowance in addition to the existing quarter/semester offered to substantial caregivers.

Significantly, in an effort to provide some relief for faculty experiencing caregiving responsibilities other than a birth/adoption event, the revisions to UC's academic policies include clarification of the part-time option for tenure-track faculty. A part-time option for UC faculty has been on the books for a number of years, but very few faculty know about it and even fewer use it. A recent inquiry sent to the campuses by UCOP regarding part-time faculty appointments found that currently the option is primarily used by male faculty who do outside consulting. The new revisions to the part-time policy make clear that the part-time option should be considered part of the package of family accommodation policies. As individual life-course needs arise—birth/adoption events, other parenting issues, personal illness, adult dependent care responsibilities, phasing into retirement—faculty could temporarily reduce the percentage time of their appointment by entering into memoranda of understanding (MOU) that would state the length and expectations of the part-time status. Data from the UC survey show that many faculty would find this option useful. As seen in Figure 1.9, women, underrepresented minorities, and assistant professors are most likely to indicate this option would be useful to them—the same groups that will make up an increasingly large share of the faculty pool in the future.

The revisions to UC's part-time policies for faculty also include materials designed to help departments and review committees grapple with the difficulties associated with reviewing faculty who are or have been part-time. Data from the UC survey indicate that our faculty are more receptive to the

FIGURE 1.9
Percent of University of California faculty indicating a flexible part-time option with pro-rated career time lines and parity* would be useful to them.

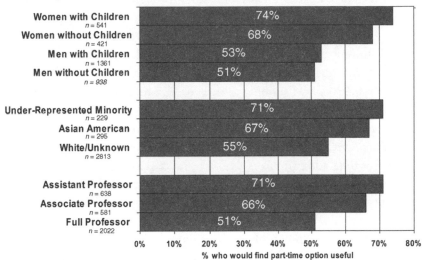

*Parity is pro-rated salary, pro-rated credit toward retirement benefits, and full health-care benefits.
Note: All differences statistically significant at *p* < *.01*.
Source: Mason, Mary Ann, Angelica Stacy, and Marc Goulden. 2003. "The UC Faculty Work and Family Survey."
(http://ucfamilyedge.berkeley.edu).

concept of prorating the career advancement *timelines* of part-time faculty than they are supportive of the idea of prorating the *quantity of research production* of part-time faculty. The policy revision underscores that expectations that part-time faculty should produce the same amount of scholarly work in the same amount of time as full-time faculty would result in part-time positions with part-time compensation but full-time expectations. Even with these difficulties, flexible part-time options for professorial series faculty are a fundamental element of a family-friendly package because caregiving can be, particularly for faculty women, a lifelong proposition.

Addressing Academic Climate Issues That May Disadvantage Faculty with Caregiving Responsibilities

Taken as a whole, UC's revised policies may well be the most generous offered by any major research university in the United States. UC's forthcoming policies have been cited as an institutional "best practice" in a recently released report at Harvard University ("Report of the Task Force," 2005). But even after these policy revisions go into effect and a publicity campaign increases faculty awareness of the policies—through Web sites, brochures, and informational packages—more work will remain. Merely increasing knowledge among faculty will not be sufficient to remedy the problems of underuse so long as many faculty fear that use will hurt their professional careers.

To help focus on institutional culture, we recommend that every campus have in place a high-level work and family advisory committee, a university work/life manager, a faculty equity officer, and annual chair orientation events. These types of institutional mechanisms serve the purpose of ensuring that frontline administrators who are directly involved with the use of family-friendly policies fully understand their appropriate use, and thus will help faculty to feel more comfortable using these policies. This is particularly important given the high turnover among chairs and the fact that chairs play a pivotal, often gatekeeping, role in the interpretation of policies.

We also recommend that scheduling of faculty meetings, classes, seminars, and receptions take into account the competing and often simultaneous demands of work and caregiving for faculty trying to excel in both realms. Whenever possible, departmental events should be scheduled between 8 a.m. and 5 p.m., regular child care provider hours, to allow faculty parents to more easily meet the dual needs of work and family. A small change of this type can have a large impact on departmental culture, feelings of inclusion among faculty, and faculty success in the academic arena.

Further cultural change in the academy is contingent on wide-scale acknowledgment and acceptance of the diversity of faculty family structures, situations, and needs. For example, dispelling myths about lack of seriousness among faculty who use tenure-clock extension to meet family needs, or nursing mothers who bring babies to conferences or presentations would go far in fostering a family-friendly culture. Review committees can also be encouraged to focus on quality of scholarly productivity rather than time since degree or job hire so that faculty who slow their career pace because of family obligations are not unduly penalized in the peer review process.

Initiatives to Improve the Career and Family Lives of UC Faculty

At UC, we are proposing a series of initiatives to address the dual-career barrier to entry into academia that women Ph.D.s are particularly likely to experience (see Figure 1.4). These include dual-career programs, relocation assistance, reentry postdoctoral appointments, and the discounting of caregiving-related résumé gaps.

The husbands or partners of women Ph.D.s are in most cases working full-time or seeking full-time professional employment. All campuses should therefore institute dual-career programs to help the working partner find appropriate career opportunities, while ensuring that women candidates are not precluded from a position because it does not meet the needs of the couple. So, too, relocation issues are of paramount importance in the recruitment of faculty. Campuses should have in place a relocation specialist who can provide faculty recruits with customized information on geographical relocation issues, referrals and resources about the nuts and bolts of a move, on- and off-campus housing, local schools, child care, elder care, recreational activities, and so on. Currently, much of this work falls to chairs, who are not trained to serve as relocation counselors, particularly given the fact that family status is legally beyond the scope of inquiry for hiring committees. Specially designed brochures made available to candidates should publicize the existence of relocation services and other family-friendly resources, policies, and resources. This would benefit recruitment and these relocation specialists could also help with retention of faculty.

For scholars who delay starting their academic careers to start families or provide care to others, it is extremely difficult to reenter academia by securing tenure-track or postdoctoral positions (see Figure 1.2). Faculty hiring committees often view such applicants as suspect because of gaps in their vitae and the time that has elapsed since they received their Ph.D.s. Campuses can set an example about the value of talented women Ph.D.s who have temporarily stepped away from the academy and combat the loss of potentially excellent scholars by encouraging faculty hiring committees to discount caregiving-related résumé gaps. Creating reentry postdoctoral positions for such candidates, such as NSF is now proposing as part of the Advance Grant initiative, can serve as a stepping-stone for Ph.D.s who need to regain currency in their discipline but are otherwise appropriate candidates.

Other university-based programs and resources are necessary to reduce the stress and work/family conflict experienced by faculty parents and caregivers, including child care and emergency/backup child care, elder/adult dependent care resources and counseling, adoption benefits, and funds for caregiving expenses related to travel. The UC survey suggests that high quality child care and infant care facilities, regular and emergency, are extremely important to faculty parents (93% of women with children and 82% of men with children would find it very or somewhat useful to them). Campuses should consider child care support to be part of the necessary infrastructure of a premier institution. If parking spaces can be considered in all new building plans, child care and infant care provisions should be part of the equation too. Facilities on or near campuses can help to minimize the time bind experienced by many faculty parents, particularly faculty mothers. Similarly, providing access to privately vendored emergency/backup child care when needed on very short notice is a low-cost way to support faculty parents in meeting the needs of work and family.

Addressing the other end of the life spectrum, a study completed in the early 1990s on the UC Berkeley campus found that 63% of UCB faculty and staff age 30 or older were either currently providing regular and ongoing assistance to an elder/adult dependent, had done so during the past five years, or expected to do so within the next five years. Many faculty, who on average begin having children in their late 30s, have to meet the complex dual needs of providing care to children and a dependent elder/adult simultaneously. Every institution should therefore have in place an elder/adult dependent care counselor to offer individual counseling, consultation and resource referrals, support groups, and informational sessions for navigating the complex issues and needs of elders or dependent adults.

Offering adoption benefits, such as reimbursement for adoption-related expenses to faculty who choose to adopt (often when delaying fertility until tenure resulted in the inability to conceive), and helping to cover the extra caregiving expenses incurred by faculty parents who must travel to professional meetings (by either bringing children with them or paying for extra care in their home), would also go a long way toward supporting the success of women academics.

Conclusion

When family-friendly policies, programs, and resources are fully in place, the academy will be better positioned to encourage women to stay in the pipeline to tenure and enjoy satisfying work and family lives as university professors. As the feminization of higher education continues, talented faculty will be drawn increasingly from the ranks of women, and institutions that ignore this basic demographic change will do so at their own peril. To attract future faculty and push gender equity forward, family-friendly initiatives are of utmost importance. For those who take note, the future holds great promise for both the institution and its faculty.

References

Armenti, C. (2004). May babies and posttenure babies: Maternal decisions of women professors. *Review of Higher Education, 27,* 211–231.

Clark, S. B. (1994). *Variations in item content and presentation in the survey of doctorate recipients, 1973–1991: Working Paper.* Washington DC: National Science Foundation.

Cole, J. R., & Zuckerman, H. (1987). Marriage, motherhood and research performance in science. *Scientific American, 255,* 119–125.

Drago, R., & Williams J. (2000). A half-time tenure track proposal. *Change, 32*(6), 46–51.

Finkel, S. K., & Olswang, S. G. (1996). Child rearing as a career impediment to women assistant professors. *Review of Higher Education, 19,* 129–139.

Ginther, D. (2001). Does science discriminate against women? Evidence from academia, 1973–97. *Working Papers 2001–2002.* Atlanta: Federal Reserve Bank of Atlanta.

Goldberger, M. L., Maher, B. A., & Flattau, P. E. (Eds.). (1995). *Research doctorate programs in the United States: Continuity and change.* Washington, DC: National Academy Press.

Hochschild, A. (1997). *The time bind: When work becomes home and home becomes work.* New York: Metropolitan Books.

Jacobs, J. (1996). Gender inequality and higher education. *Annual Review of Sociology, 22,* 153–85.

Kulis, S., Sicotte, D., & Collins, S. (2002). More than a pipeline problem: Labor supply constraints and gender stratification across academic science disciplines. *Research in Higher Education, 43,* 657–691.

Long, J. S. (Ed.). (2001). *From scarcity to visibility: Gender differences in the careers of doctoral scientists and engineers.* Washington, DC: National Academy Press.

Long, J. S., Allison, P. D., & McGinnis, R. (1993). Rank advancement in academic careers: Sex differences and the effects of productivity. *American Sociological Review, 58,* 703–722.

Mason, M. A., & Goulden, M. (2002, November–December). Do babies matter?: The effect of family formation on the lifelong careers of academic men and women. *Academe, 88*(6), 21–27.

Mason, M. A., & Goulden, M. (2004a, November–December). Do babies matter? (Part 2): Closing the baby gap. *Academe, 90*(6), 3–7.

Mason, M. A., & Goulden, M. (2004b, November). Marriage and baby blues: Redefining gender equity in the academy. *Annals of the American Academy of Political and Social Science, 596,* 86–103.

Mason, M. A., Stacy, A., & Goulden, M. (2003). *The UC faculty work and family survey.* Berkeley: University of California.

National Center for Education Statistics. (2003a). *The integrated postsecondary education data system (IPEDS) completions survey, Fall 2002 survey.* Washington, DC: Author.

National Center for Education Statistics. (2003b). *The integrated postsecondary education data system (IPEDS) salaries, tenure, and fringe benefits survey, Fall 1999 survey.* Washington, DC: Author.

National Science Foundation. (1995). *Changes to the survey of doctorate recipients in 1991 and 1993: Implications for data users.* Arlington, VA: Author.

National Science Foundation. (2004a). *Gender differences in the careers of academic scientists and engineers,* NSF 04–323, Project Officer, Alan I. Rapoport. Arlington, VA: Author.

National Science Foundation. (2004b). Survey of Doctorate Recipients. http://www.nsf.gov/sbe/srs/ssdr/start.htm

National Science Foundation. (2004c). Survey of Earned Doctorates. http://www.nsf.gov/sbe/srs/sed/start.htm

Perna, L. (2001). Sex and race differences in faculty tenure and promotion. *Research in Higher Education, 42,* 541–567.

Report of the task force on women faculty. (2005, May). Harvard University. Retrieved December 6, 2005, from http://www.news.harvard.edu/gazette/daily/2005/05/women-faculty.pdf

Toutkoushian, R. (1999). The status of academic women in the 1990s: No longer outsiders, but not yet equals. *Quarterly Review of Economics and Finance, 39,* 679–698.

Valian, V. (1998). *Why so slow?: The advancement of women.* Cambridge, Mass.: MIT Press.

Varner, A. (2000). *The consequences and costs of delaying attempted childbirth for women faculty.* University Park: Department of Labor Studies and Industrial Relations, Pennsylvania State University.

Williams, J. (2000). *Unbending gender: Why family and work conflict and what to do about it.* Oxford, UK: Oxford University Press.

Wolfinger, N. H., Mason, M. A., & Goulden, M. (2004). *Problems in the pipeline: Gender, marriage, and fertility in the ivory tower.* Paper presented at the annual meeting of the American Sociological Association, San Francisco.

Xie, Y., & Shauman, K. A. (1998). Sex differences in research productivity: New evidence about an old puzzle. *American Sociological Review, 63,* 847–870.

Notes

1. Thanks to the Association of Institutional Researchers and the Alfred P. Sloan Foundation for funding our research; and Angelica Stacy, Carol Hoffman, and Karie Frasch who worked with us on parts of this analysis. The use of National Science Foundation data does not imply NSF endorsement of research methods or conclusions contained in this report.

2. Rankings are based on the National Research Council's ranks as reported in Goldberger, Maher, and Flattau (1995).

3. We converted the findings from these two regression models (Wolfinger, Mason, & Goulden, 2004) to predicted probabilities for the two-career outcomes, tenure-track entry, and tenure.

4. For a copy of complete regression results, please contact Marc Goulden (goulden@berkeley.edu).

5. For a copy of complete regression results, please contact Marc Goulden (goulden@berkeley.edu).

6. For a copy of complete regression results, please contact Marc Goulden (goulden@berkeley.edu).

7. For a copy of complete regression results, please contact Marc Goulden (goulden@berkeley.edu).

8. Special thanks to Robert Drago, who initially developed a number of these survey questions as part of his Mapping Project (http://lsir.la.psu.edu/workfam/prelimresults.htm).

9. The proposed revisions are posted at the following University of California Office of the President (UCOP) Web site: http://www.ucop.edu/acadadv/acadpers/apm/review.html

2

HOW FEMALE AND MALE FACULTY WITH FAMILIES MANAGE WORK AND PERSONAL ROLES

Carol L. Colbeck

Now mother Vanessa Lynch and single father James Cary are among the many faculty who juggle their roles as tenure-line faculty members and parents.[1] One evening, for example, a colleague came to Vanessa's home to collaborate on a research project. Vanessa, an associate professor of English, simultaneously prepared dinner, kept her eye on her nine-month-old baby, and discussed research ideas with her colleague. On another afternoon, assistant professor of English James Cary was at home drinking coffee and reading an article related to his current writing project when his younger child arrived home and asked to attend a talent show at her school that evening. James called the school to verify details about the talent show, then spent the next 12 minutes talking with his daughter about her day, schoolwork, and plans for the evening. The assistant professor read the article for another seven minutes until his teenager blew in, and James chatted with her for a couple of minutes before tidying the kitchen. He went upstairs to work on his paper, but it was only a couple of minutes before his younger daughter asked if she could bring a friend to the talent show. For the next hour, James shifted back and forth between editing his article for a few minutes at a time, responding to his daughters' requests, and household chores. These examples show how work and family frequently overlapped for Vanessa and James. If given the chance, both said they would decrease the separation between the two domains even more. James also wished for more time just for himself and to engage in activities unrelated to either work or family.

In contrast to Vanessa and James, some faculty members deliberately separate their parent and work roles. Even though his wife worked as a technician in assistant professor Chris Ewing's chemistry department, he said that they "never talk about [work] stuff at home and vice-versa." Similarly, assistant professor of chemistry Michelle Fisher came to realize that "what was best for me is that I do have to segregate my time between 'this is work time' and 'this is family time.'" When she went home after a day in the lab, Michelle often supported her stay-at-home husband's desires to take a break, and she took over care of their preschooler while he went out for a while. Asked to imagine a more ideal allocation of time, Michelle indicated she was satisfied with the current arrangement. Chris said, however, that he would prefer to spend more time with his family and less time at work.

On average, college and university tenure-line faculty work long hours, even faculty like Vanessa, James, Chris, and Michelle who have children living at home. The average work week reported by assistant professors with children in the United States was 56.3 hours for men and 52.5 hours for women in the most recent National Survey of Postsecondary Faculty (Jacobs & Winslow, 2003). In addition, professors living with children work a second shift at home (Hochschild, 1989). Individuals' attempts to meet others' and their own expectations in both domains can result in a sense of conflict between work and family domains. Because women typically assume more dependent care responsibilities than men, expectations abound that female faculty allow family to interfere with work more, and are therefore less productive than male faculty. Perhaps because of family responsibilities, there are more women in part-time, nontenured, and lower tenure-line faculty ranks than men (Perna, 2001). A recent national study found, however, when controlling for rank, family members, and discipline, research productivity is nearly equivalent between the sexes (Sax, Hagedorn, Marriscol, & DiCrisi, 2002).

Perception of conflict is often based on the assumption that "time spent on activities within one role generally cannot be devoted to activities within another role" (Greenhaus & Beutell, 1985, p. 77). The opposite of work/family conflict is often characterized by work/family scholars as "balance," or being equally involved in and satisfied with work family roles (Greenhaus & Singh, 2003). Some scholars, such as Rapoport, Bailyn, Fletcher, and Pruitt (2002), assert that giving equal weight to personal and professional life is not necessarily optimal for every individual. They prefer the term "integration," and define it as functioning well and finding satisfaction in both work and personal life, regardless of how much time is actually spent in each domain. Integration also connotes diminishing "the separation between these two spheres of life in ways that will change both" (Rapoport et al., 2002, p. 36).

Although work/family scholars frequently discuss time as an essential contributor to perceptions of conflict, balance, or integration, they have failed to measure time use in ways that would actually determine the extent to which individuals actually "diminish the separation" between work and family domains. Instead, researchers have either assessed individual perceptions of time-based conflict or their self-reported allocation of time to work and family as separate and distinct domains. Perceptions of time-based conflict have been assessed from individuals' responses to survey questions asking to what degree individuals feel so tired from work or family responsibilities that they are less able to deal with duties in the other domain (Jacobs & Gerson, 2004; Roehling, Moen, & Batt, 2003). The finding of a null relationship between work and family concerns may imply that individuals are separating the two domains (Judge & Watanabe, 1994). Clark (2000) points out that such research is limited because it focuses primarily on "emotional linkages" and does not acknowledge the "spatial, temporal, social, and behavioral connections between work and family" (pp. 749–750).

Prior studies that investigated allocation of time to work and family also fail to deal with temporal connections between the two domains. These studies typically ask participants to report the number of hours per week spent at work and on specified personal activities such as household chores, child care, shopping, and household maintenance (Clarkberg & Merola, 2003; Fox & Dwyer, 1999; Gutek, Searle, & Klepa, 1991; O'Driscoll, Ilgen, & Hildreth, 1992). Researchers expected to find large and significant negative correlations between work time and personal time because "the amount of time devoted to one domain should reduce time available for the other" (O'Driscoll et al., 1992, p. 274). Results, however, range from zero (Clarkberg & Merola, 2003) to "only − .38" (O'Driscoll et al., 1992). One reason the researchers may have failed to find that nonwork time was roughly equivalent to personal time could be that time spent in one domain is sometimes also time spent in the other domain. Vanessa demonstrated this when simultaneously caring for her baby, cooking dinner, and discussing research with a colleague.

The study described in this chapter challenges the notion that time spent in paid work is necessarily time *not* devoted to personal or family activities. Further, I suggest that the concept of integration of work and personal life as defined by Rapoport et al. (2002) should be expanded to include time, specifically the instances when individuals fulfill expectations of two or more roles at the same time. This study explored work-personal integration for tenure-line faculty at research universities by seeking answers to the following questions: (1) For what proportion of their waking time do female and male faculty with families integrate their work and personal roles by accomplishing goals from each domain simultaneously? (2) How flexible and permeable are the boundaries that female and male faculty members maintain between their work and personal roles? (3) How satisfied are female and male faculty with their allocation of time to work and family roles and with their own level of work-personal integration?

Conceptual Foundations

Role theory and its variants, border and boundary theories, provide the conceptual foundation for this analysis. A role is the set of behaviors expected of a specific office or position (Sarbin & Allen, 1968), and an individual in a single position can perform multiple roles (Katz & Kahn, 1966). Traditional role theory suggests that performing one role results in a net loss of time and energy, and performing multiple roles leads to depletion and stress. Marks (1977), however, questioned why a sizable minority of individuals who perform multiple roles do not feel drained of time and energy. He implied that some individuals may find time to fulfill multiple roles by doing two or more things at once.

Integration involves engaging in activities that simultaneously satisfy expectations for two or more roles (Colbeck, 1998). A few studies have investigated the percent of work time in which faculty accomplish multiple work goals at the same time. For example, in a pilot workload study at Arizona State University, humanities, social science, and science faculty reported that they integrated teaching and research 12.9%, 16.8%, and 18.0% of their work time, respectively (Krahenbuhl, 1998). I documented similar overlaps between faculty work roles when I conducted structured observations of 12 physicists' and English professors' work activities at two universities (Colbeck, 1998, 2001). During more than 1,000 hours that I observed the 12 male full professors, they integrated teaching and research 18.8%, research and service 7.5%, and teaching and service 5.7% of their work time, on average.

A few scholars have explored the notion of integration or blurring of boundaries between work and personal roles. Both boundary theory (Ashforth, Kreiner, & Fugate, 2000; Nippert-Eng, 1996) and work/family border theory (Clark, 2000) explore how individuals transition between roles. The boundaries or borders between work and family may be physical, temporal, or psychological. The relative ease of navigating between work and family domains is influenced by the flexibility and permeability of the barriers between them.

Flexibility is the extent to which barriers are malleable, allowing one role to accommodate the demands of another role. Clark provides the following examples: "If individuals are free to work any hours they choose, the temporal border separating work and family is very flexible. If individuals may work in any location they choose, the physical border is very flexible" (2000, p. 757). Degree of flexibility may be determined by conditions of employment. Shift workers, for example, have little flexibility. For academics, however, maintaining flexible boundaries between work and family is often a matter of personal choice. Vanessa Lynch considered the barriers between work and family domains as flexible enough to conduct research during the dinner hour at home with a colleague while attending to her baby. In contrast, Chris Ewing felt comfortable maintaining inflexible barriers between work and family by choosing not to discuss work at home or home at work with his wife who worked in the same department.

Permeability involves the degree to which role barriers may be penetrated for interruptions. According to Ashforth et al. (2000), "an employee who is able to accept personal calls and visits regularly has a permeable work role boundary" (p. 474). Not only did James Cary maintain a flexible boundary between work and family domains by working often at home, this boundary was quite permeable as he shifted back and forth frequently between conversations with his daughters and writing an article for publication. Michelle Fisher, on the other hand, found it easier to maintain less permeable boundaries between work and family. Once home, she engaged fully with her toddler. She also asked her husband to refrain from leaving their son with her in the lab during the day because she was unable to do her chemistry research while simultaneously attending to an inquisitive two-year-old. As with flexibility, faculty members have more control over the permeability of their work/family boundaries than many other workers.

This study also explored individual faculty members' *satisfaction* with their own patterns for allocation of time and integration of roles. Previous studies have investigated either the difference between actual and ideal time allocated to paid work or the difference between actual and ideal integration (or its opposite, segmentation) of work and family domains. A majority of workers, but especially highly educated and well-paid professionals, say they would prefer to allocate less time than they actually do to paid work (Clarkberg and Merola, 2003; Jacobs & Gerson, 2004). Edwards and Rothbard (2000) investigated the fit between actual and ideal segmentation of work and personal domains for university employees. They found that a good fit between actual and preferred segmentation was associated with more work and family satisfaction and less anxiety and depression.

Gender may influence the extent to which faculty integrate work and personal roles, maintain permeable or flexible boundaries between them, or perceive differences between their actual and ideal allocation of time and role integration. Women tend to spend more time on family duties than men. A national time diary study of a cross section of the population revealed that, on average, employed women dedicate 25.6 hours per week to household work, including 13 hours in child care, while employed men devote about 14.5 hours per week in household work, 11 of which are spent on child care (Robinson, 1997). Furthermore, a survey of 184 dual-career faculty families shows that even when faculty wives earn more than their husbands, the wives reported spending more time on household chores than their husbands (Rhoads & Rhoads, 2003). Studies that have investigated the relationship of gender to perceived work/family conflict yielded mixed results with some reporting higher levels of conflict for women than men (Gutek et al., 1991), higher levels for men than women (Eagle, Icenogle, Maes, & Miles, 1998), or little difference between men and women (Frone, Russell, & Barnes, 1996).

Methods

This study combined structured observations to ascertain empirically the extent to which female and male faculty with dependent children accomplish work and family goals at the same time with interviews to understand why they integrate or segment their roles and how they feel about it. The sample of 13 faculty members from two research-extensive universities included 1 full, 6 associate, and 6 assistant professors. Participants were almost evenly divided by sex (7 women and 6 men) and by discipline (6 faculty from English departments and 7 from chemistry or chemistry-related departments).

Data collection with each participant involved an initial interview, three nonconsecutive days of structured observation over the course of an academic year, and a final interview. The first interview elicited information about participants' work responsibilities, schedule, and environment, family responsibilities, schedule, and fit between actual and ideal allocation of time and role integration. During 303.2 hours of structured observations (Mintzberg, 1973), the author or one of two assistants shadowed participants from the time they left for work in the morning until the early evening hours. According to Jacobs and Gerson, "Observational studies, in which an unbiased observer reports on what is really happening at the workplace or around the kitchen table, offer a way to circumvent the potential distortions of self-reports" (2004, p. 15). Observers noted a description and the duration of each activity to the nearest minute. To gain complete information about all activities in every participant's day, we asked them to record detailed time diaries about all their activities from 5:00 p.m. the night before until the start of the observation in the morning. Participants also shared general goal and aspect information about confidential work activities when the observer should not be present, such as faculty meetings or counseling appointments with individual students. The data include 340.8 hours of immediately reported activities. Finally, questions from the concluding interviews elicited participants' perceptions of interrole conflict as well as integration of their work and family roles.

Faculty activity data were entered in an Excel database, with a record for each of 4,929 discrete activities. Activity goals were coded as Administration, Graduate Education, Undergraduate Education, Research, Service, Commute, General Work, and Personal. Defining aspects of each goal were also coded. For example, activities that met Personal goals included household work, dependent care, obtaining goods and services, personal needs and care, personal growth, organizational, entertainment/social, recreation, communications, and religious activity. Activities that fulfilled more than one goal were coded for all appropriate goals and aspects. For example, when Sarah

Levin ate lunch while discussing general research issues with colleagues and a visiting scholar, the activity was coded as [GOAL = Personal; ASPECT = Personal Needs and Care] and [GOAL = Research; ASPECT = Scholarship]. When Ingrid Holbrooke walked her children to school on her way to her lab in the morning, we coded the time until after the good-bye kisses as [GOAL = Personal; ASPECT = Dependent Care] and [GOAL = Commute]. Activities were also coded for the location where they took place, such as home, office, department, car, or community.

We calculated the sum of minutes and the proportion of total waking time[2] that each faculty member allocated to each goal and aspect. For the purpose of analysis for this study, work goals (research, undergraduate and graduate education, administration, service) were combined into a single "Work" role category. Similarly, any action that involved caring for children was coded as "Dependent Care," and any personal action that did not involve responsibility for children was coded as "Other Personal." Each participant spent some time solely explaining their activities to the observer; we coded these activities as "Talking with Observer." This time is a good indication of the extent to which participants modified their activities during the study as a consequence of being observed.

To ascertain satisfaction with allocation of time and role integration, we asked each participant to draw two Venn diagrams with four circles representing work, family, self, and other community activities. The size of the circles represented the average amount of time devoted to each domain; the degree of overlap between circles represented the extent to which they integrated activities from two or more domains. Participants' first drawings depicted their current average allocation of time and integration of roles; their second drawings depicted their ideal allocation of time and role integration.

Integration

When faculty members integrate their personal and professional roles, they accomplish personal and work goals at the same time. There are two forms of integration. The first occurs when an individual engages in a single activity that meets both personal and work goals, as when associate professor of chemistry Heidi Gold discussed research over lunch with her husband who was also a department colleague. She said during an interview, "My husband and I have lunch together at least two or three, four times a week sometimes.

So the fact that we manage to get some family in at work and our fields are similar enough that we do talk about work a lot. So in fact there's a major overlap between family and work in that we're both in similar fields and science goes on at home, too." The second form, sometimes called multi-tasking, occurs when individuals may engage in two activities simultaneously, one of which accomplishes a personal goal while the other meets a professional goal. Vanessa Lynch did so when she nursed her baby while reading a draft of a student's thesis. Regardless of the form, the extent to which individuals simultaneously accomplish personal and professional goals provides one indicator of the degree of separation they maintain between the two domains.

The average number of hours and percent of waking time women and men participants allocated to work and personal activities during the study are shown in Table 2.1. The women engaged in work activities (graduate or undergraduate education, research, administration, service, or general work) and commuting an average of nearly 10 hours per day, an amount equivalent to 57.3% of their waking time. They also spent an average of 8 hours and 39 minutes, or 50.1%, of their waking time in dependent care and other personal

TABLE 2.1
Allocation of Time to Work, Commute, and Personal Purposes
Aggregated by Gender

Personal and Work Roles	Women		Men	
	Average Hrs/Day	*% Awake Time*	*Average Hrs/Day*	*% Awake Time*
Work	8:56	51.7	9:20	56.2
Commute	0:58	5.6	0:56	5.7
Total Work	9:54	57.3	10:16	61.9
Dependent Care	4:17	24.8	2:44	16.5
Other Personal	4:22	25.3	5:08	31.0
Total Personal	8:39	50.1	7:52	47.5
Talk with observer	0:20	1.9	0:31	3.1
TOTAL (with integration)	18:53	109.3	18:39	112.5
Integrated Work and Personal	1:36	9.3	2:04	12.5
TOTAL (unduplicated)	17:17	100.0	16:35	100.0

activities. For 20 minutes per day, on average, women did nothing else but talk to the researchers observing their activities. During the 17 hours and 17 minutes of their total average time awake each day, the women integrated their work and personal roles for 1 hour and 36 minutes, or 9.3%, of their waking time. One woman integrated her work and personal roles much more than the others. Vanessa Lynch simultaneously accomplished work and personal goals 20.4% of her waking time. Work-personal integration for the other 6 women ranged from 4.5% for chemist Michelle Fisher to 10.6% for chemist Ingrid Holbrooke.

The men participants spent slightly more time on work, much less time on dependent care, and integrated work and personal roles somewhat more than the women. Men spent an average of 10 hours and 16 minutes, or 61.9%, of their waking time each day engaged in work activities or commuting. Dependent care and other personal activities took nearly 8 hours, or 47.5%, of their waking time per day. Men spent an average 31 minutes per observation day engaged solely in talking with the researchers observing their activities. The men integrated personal and work roles just over two hours, or 12.5% of the average 16 hours and 35 minutes they were awake and active during the average day. One man integrated his work and personal roles much less than others. Chemist Chris Ewing, who deliberately tried to segregate work and personal domains, integrated them only 4.7% of his waking time, while the other five men integrated work and personal roles between 11.1% and 16.8% of their waking time.

There were some interesting differences in the ways that men and women integrated their work and personal roles. Not only did women spend more time than men on dependent care, women also integrated dependent care with their work and commute more than twice as much: 3.7% compared to 1.6% of waking time, on average. Heidi Gold, for example, invited her teenage daughter to help create a poster for a department function. Both men and women combined work and personal roles when they ate at their desks, discussed work over lunch or during racquetball games with colleagues, hosted social events for students or colleagues, or talked about their families at work. Some of the women participants, in fact, perceived that they served as role models for combining work and family when they talked about family with graduate students. Sarah Levin said, "I've always discussed my family life with my graduate students. I don't like feel like I have to partition that off." The men participants, however, spent more time integrating work with some form of personal communication than women. Communication was defined for this study as "listening to the radio, watching television, reading a book or magazine, having a conversation with another about personal issues." Men integrated work with personal communication 4.5% of their waking time, while only 1.2% of the women's waking time was spent in work and personal communication. Much of the communication time for both men and women involved personal conversations with colleagues throughout the work day. Some men also combined work and personal communication in other ways, such as when Jim Sheverelle and his wife planned for her to serve as guest lecturer in his undergraduate class, and Lewis Greene watched films at home relevant to courses he taught.

Flexibility

Boundaries or borders between work and family are flexible to the extent that hours and locations of either may be varied easily (Clark, 2000). Flexibility of work physical boundaries was assessed for this analysis by measuring the percent of time faculty engaged in work activities at home. Similarly the flexibility of home boundaries was measured by the percent of time faculty engaged in personal activities on campus. Commuting was omitted from this analysis because all but two participants commuted by car. Roger Pauling ran home from work two times, and Ingrid Holbrooke often walked to and from work.

The percent of waking time and the locations where women and men faculty engaged in activities that were solely personal, solely work, or that integrated their work and personal roles are shown in Table 2.2. Men engaged in work activities at home for a higher percent of their waking time than women. Men engaged in activities that were focused solely on work or that integrated work and personal roles for a total of 15% of their waking time. In contrast, women participants spent only 5.9% of their waking time at home on work or integrated work-personal activities. Women also spent somewhat more time at home focused entirely on personal and family issues (32.7%) than did men (29.3%). Thus, men's family boundaries were more flexible than women's for accommodating work.

Work boundaries were also somewhat more flexible for accommodating personal activities for men than for women. Activities that were purely personal or that integrated work and personal roles engaged women for only

TABLE 2.2
Location of Personal and Work Activities as Percent of Waking Time

	Women			Men		
	Personal Only	*Work/ Personal*	*Work Only*	*Personal Only*	*Work/ Personal*	*Work Only*
Home	32.7	2.5	3.4	29.3	3.6	11.4
Campus	1.6	2.9	39.7	2.0	4.8	33.9
Car	1.0	0.1	0.2	0.6	0	0
Community	5.5	1.9	1.0	3.0	1.8	0.8

4.5% of their time in their offices, labs, departments, or elsewhere on campus. Men spent 6.8% of their time on campus doing things that met solely personal goals or integrated work and personal goals. The women faculty observed for this study spent a higher percent of their waking time on campus solely focused on work (39.7%) than did the men (33.9%).

Men allowed more flexibility in their home boundaries than in their work boundaries. They worked at home more than twice as much as they engaged in personal activities at work. Women maintained stronger physical boundaries between work and home boundaries than men in both domains. In fact, the women's most flexible boundary, accommodating work at home, was less flexible than the men's least flexible boundary, accommodating personal in the workplace.

Permeability

Work or family boundaries are permeable to the extent that activities from one domain may easily or frequently interrupt activities in the other. Permeability varied among participants as well as for each participant, depending on task and location. When Ingrid Holbrooke focused intently on work in her chemistry lab, she maintained a boundary that was quite impermeable to personal interruption. During lunch with a department colleague who also had school-age children, however, Ingrid's work boundary became very permeable as conversation bounced back and forth between talk of soccer practice, graduate assistant recruitment, summer camps, and department politics. In contrast, when English associate professor Lewis Greene wrote at home for almost four hours straight, his home boundary flexibly accommodated work, but was relatively impermeable because he allowed himself almost no personal interruptions.

On average, men participants' home boundaries were far more permeable to work than the women participants' home boundaries, as shown in Table 2.3. During the study, a total of 622 activities were recorded as done by the men at home. Of these, 171, or 27.5%, of the activities done at home fulfilled either solely work goals or integrated work and personal goals. Of the total of 543 activities recorded at home for women participants, only 59, or 10.9 %, of the activities were related to their work. This indicates that the men faculty allowed work activities to interrupt home activities two and half times more often than did the women faculty.

Laurel Sun's and Jim Sheverelle's comments illuminate the difference. Both are associate professors of English, parents of preschoolers, and have spouses with full-time professional careers. Laurel described how her young family demands her attention at home, making work there nearly impossible. "When I'm at home either with them wholly or even with my husband, there is no way [the children] will not come seek me out and seek my attention and that goes for my husband as well." In contrast, Jim said, "because I work at home a lot, I make the distinction between work and home evaporate in many ways because I do so much of my work at home. I never really feel like okay, I'm home now, I'm done with work. Or I have an hour here, I'll go sit down and work on some e-mails to people on my committee about X, Y and Z, you know. That line between getting off work and going home doesn't exist. And sometimes I think that's a bad thing."

Women's work boundaries were almost as permeable to personal inter-

TABLE 2.3
Location and Number of Personal and Work Activities

	Women			Men		
	Personal Only	Work/ Personal	Work Only	Personal Only	Work/ Personal	Work Only
Home	484	33	26	451	30	141
Campus	80	154	1285	72	208	1388
Car	28	2	4	25	1	0
Community	79	35	14	23	31	5

ruptions as men's work boundaries. Men engaged in 280 personal activities or integrated work-personal activities out of a total of 1,668 activities recorded in their offices, labs, classrooms, departments, or other facilities on campus. Thus, 16.8% of their on campus activities were directed entirely or partially toward a personal goal. Of the total 1,519 activities recorded on campus for women, 234, or 15.4%, were solely personal or integrated work and personal goals.

Although the women allowed slightly fewer personal interruptions at work than men, personal activities interrupted women's work on campus more than work activities permeated their personal lives at home. In contrast, men's work boundaries were much less permeable than their home boundaries.

Satisfaction

More women than men participants were satisfied with their current allocation of time to work and personal activities. In fact, when asked to draw pictures of their actual and ideal time allocation and integration of activities involving work, family, self, and community activities, 3 of the 7 women said their current actual was already close to ideal. Chemist Heidi Gold said she "may not change much. Maybe it's because I feel like it is working, so don't mess with it." Michelle Fisher was comfortable with the choices she and her husband made together about work and family for the moment. She said, "I'm lucky in that my husband's home and that allows me to really be able to do both of these things—take care of my family well, and at the same time, spend the time I need to be successful at work." Ingrid Holbrooke said, "The only way you can make ideal better [than actual] would be to add more hours in the day and just make all the circles bigger. But I think the ratio of circles to each other would stay about the same."

The other 4 women indicated they would maintain approximately the same allocation of time to work and family roles, but would prefer to integrate them more. Ironically, Vanessa Lynch initially said that she would like to integrate her roles more. Observations revealed, however, that she integrated work and personal more than any other participant in the study. At her final interview, she also recognized that "I'm often doing more than one thing at a time. That's what this study made me realize. It's rare that I'm just doing one thing at a time." Lynn Johnson, Sarah Levin, and Laurel Sun also voiced desire for more overlap between work and family because, as Laurel said, "that relationship between work and family is a good one and it works for me." Laurel added, however, that she wished for more time just for herself. Sarah also said, "I don't have a whole huge personal life that's outside my family."

The men participants voiced less satisfaction than the women with their current allocation of time and integration of work and personal roles. Only Lewis Greene's drawings of his actual and ideal allocation of time were nearly identical. Matthew Park, Chris Ewing, and Jim Sheverelle said that ideally, they would devote more time to family and less time to work. Chemist Matthew said, "All I do is I just come to the department and then go home to some food and then sleep. That's all I do." While he and his wife agree that long work hours were necessary at this point in his career, Matthew knew that both his wife and his children would like to see more of him. Similarly, Jim said that he and his wife would "like for the family time to be larger than the work time. But I just don't see how that's going to happen." Jim also wanted more separation between family and work. James Cary and Roger Pauling not only wanted more time for themselves, they also wanted to be more involved in the community. As Roger said, "I've always been very politically involved and involved in a lot of things and I just don't have the time to do it now."

Summary and Discussion

The findings from this study provide evidence that linkages between work and personal roles can be measured in terms of time and location as well as in terms of emotional perceptions. While the male participants spent somewhat more time on work and less time on personal activities than the female participants, their work and family roles were not mutually exclusive. Time spent on work was, in fact, occasionally also time devoted to family, self, or community. Faculty participants integrated their work with their personal roles by engaging in activities that accomplished both goals simultaneously more than 10%, on average, of their waking time recorded for this study. Most of the male faculty integrated work and personal roles slightly more than the women faculty. The women faculty on the whole, however, felt that their actual allocation of time and integration of roles were close to ideal. In contrast, most of the male faculty indicated that, ideally, they would work less, spend more time with family, and segment their work and family roles more.

With its small sample, this study can only begin to explore the relationship between patterns of time allocation and role integration. Most women in this sample were satisfied with their comparatively small integration of roles; most of the men expressed desires to reduce their comparatively larger work-personal role integration. However, the individual who integrated work and personal roles more than any other participant in the study was Vanessa Lynch, and she was satisfied as she came to recognize how much she accomplished work and personal goals simultaneously. Similarly, the individual who integrated work and personal roles less than other participants was Chris Ewing. While he said he would prefer to reallocate his time between work and family roles, he was satisfied with the segmentation he maintained between them. This indicates that individual preference as well as gender may affect overall satisfaction with work-personal time allocation and role integration. Edwards and Rothbard (2000) found that university employees who said they segmented their work lives and preferred segmentation reported a greater degree of overall well-being than those who said they integrated their work and personal lives and preferred integration.

The male participants in this study maintained more flexible and permeable boundaries around their work and family roles both at home and on campus than the female faculty. In particular, the men spent more than twice as much time engaged in work activities at home than women. They also allowed work activities to interrupt personal and family activities at home far more often than did the women. Both male and female participants maintained stronger boundaries around their work on campus than they did around personal activities at home. Work boundaries were less flexible and less permeable, however, to personal time and interruption for the women than for the men. These findings contradict assumptions that women faculty allow family to interfere with work more than men faculty do.

Faculty members have more discretion than workers in many other jobs and professions regarding how to plan their days (Roehling et al., 2003). Many of the participants in this study appreciated the flexibility and permeability inherent in their faculty jobs. Jim Sheverelle, Roger Pauling, Sarah Levin, and Heidi Gold talked of the freedom they had to take children to doctor and dentist appointments without the need to make special arrangements at work. Lynn Johnson, Vanessa Lynch, Laurel Sun, and Ingrid Holbrooke were able to arrange weekly course schedules so they and their husbands were able to alternate days for leaving work early so one parent was available to care for the children after school or day care.

While faculty may have much discretion over their allocation of time and integration of roles, those seeking advancement also work under tremendous pressure to meet high, but often unclearly specified, expectations for tenure or promotion. Faculty, like many other professionals, try to live up to the norm of the "ideal worker," someone who enters a profession immediately upon receiving the relevant academic credential, works his or her way up the career ladder by putting in long hours without interruptions beyond short vacations, and continues in this fashion until retirement age (Williams, 1999).

With the combination of discretion and pressure to meet professional expectations, faculty members have "the freedom to work themselves to death," as one of my colleagues once observed. Some faculty seem to realize more than others that they actually choose how they respond to the pressure and how they allocate time to work, family, self, and community. For English professor Jim Sheverelle, the pressure manifested in a constant feeling that work was never done. "I could put as many hours into this job as I could find time to do because there's always something else I haven't written, or something else I haven't taken care of yet. Whereas if I worked a nine to six kind of job in which when I got off at six I would have every evening to do whatever I wanted to." Chemist Roger Pauling resisted such pressure and insisted on keeping an "8:30 to 5:00 Monday to Friday schedule" unlike his "normal schedule" when he was a single graduate student, which "was more on the order of 90 to a hundred hours a week, seven days a week." Roger now wanted to spend mornings, nights, and weekends with his wife and preschooler.

Faculty may not realize the extent to which they choose how much they integrate or segment their roles, and how much flexibility and permeability they allow in the boundaries between their work and personal roles. Simple awareness can make a difference and help faculty make conscious choices that work well for them. As a result of participating in the study, Vanessa Lynch realized, "It's rare that I'm just doing one thing at a time," and she was comfortable with the extent of her role integration.

Colleagues and administrators can help by expressing better understanding and support of faculty parents' multiple roles. Heidi Gold appreciated efforts along these lines made by an associate dean.

> She's always asking, well, what can we do to get more faculty activities and get people out to things? Ironically, the one thing I could think of is, do more family things. Have family get-togethers where the family is invited, not just faculty members, but make it more family oriented so it's understood that we are families. We have families and they're part of our lives. They're not something that we partition off a hundred percent into a different sphere. She being a mom and everything, she kind of picked up on that.

Chemist Roger Pauling thought universities should realize "it's worth investing the energy of hiring people who have families that are big parts of their lives into these types of positions because we make probably well-informed and balanced decisions about the types of things that we want to work on. So it's not a problem having a family; it's really an asset." He wanted policy set "such that faculty members with family are just as cherished as faculty members that are spending 150 hours a week pounding away at their work."

References

Ashforth, B. E., Kreiner, G. E., & Fugate, M. (2000). All in a day's work: Boundaries and micro role transitions. *Academy of Management Review, 25*(3), 472–491.

Clark, S. C. (2000). Work/family border theory: A new theory of work/family balance. *Human Relations, 53*(6), 747–770.

Clarkberg, M., & Merola, S. S. (2003). Competing clocks: Work and Leisure. In P. Moen (Ed.), *It's about time: Couples and careers* (pp. 35–48). Ithaca, NY: Cornell University Press.

Colbeck, C. L. (1998). Merging in a seamless blend: How faculty integrate teaching and research. *Journal of Higher Education, 69*(6), 647–667.

Colbeck, C. L. (2001). Integration: Evaluating faculty work as a whole. In C. L. Colbeck (Ed.), *Evaluating faculty performance* (pp. 43–52). San Francisco: Jossey-Bass.

Eagle, B. W., Icenogle, M. L., Maes, J. D., & Miles, E. W. (1998). The importance of employee demographic profiles for understanding experiences of work-family interrole conflicts. *Journal of Social Psychology, 138*(6), 690–709.

Edwards, J. R., & Rothbard, N. P. (2000). Mechanisms linking work and family:

Clarifying the relationship between work and family constructs. *Academy of Management Review, 25*(1), 178–199.

Fox, M. L., & Dwyer, D. J. (1999). An investigation of the effects of time and involvement in the relationship between stressors and work-family conflict. *Journal of Occupational Health Psychology, 4,* 164–174.

Frone, M. R., Russell, M., & Barnes, G. M. (1996). Work-family conflict, gender, and health-related outcomes: A study of employed parents in two community samples. *Journal of Occupational Health Psychology, 1,* 57–67.

Greenhaus, J. H., & Beutell, N. J. (1985). Sources of conflict between work and family roles. *Academy of Management Review, 10*(1), 76–88.

Greenhaus, J. H., & Singh, R. (2003). Work-family linkages. A Sloan Work and Family Encyclopedia entry. Retrieved December 7, 2005, from http://wfnet work.bc.edu/encyclopedia_entry.php?id = 263

Gutek, B. A., Searle, S., & Klepa, L. (1991). Rational versus gender role explanations of work-family conflict. *Journal of Applied Psychology, 76*(4), 560–568.

Hochschild, A. (1989). *The second shift: Working parents and the revolution at home.* New York: Viking Press.

Jacobs, J. A., & Gerson, K. (2004). *The time divide: Work, family, and gender inequality.* Cambridge, MA: Harvard University Press.

Jacobs, J. A., & Winslow, S. E. (2003, July). *The academic life course, time pressures, and gender equity.* Paper presented at the Association of American University Professors Symposium on Work/Family Issues, Washington, DC.

Judge, T. A., & Watanabe, S. (1994). Individual differences in the nature of the relationship between job and life satisfaction. *Journal of Occupational and Organizational Psychology, 67,* 101–107.

Katz, D. & Kahn, R. L. (1966). *The social psychology of organizations.* New York: Wiley.

Krahenbuhl, G. S. (1998). Faculty work: Integrating responsibilities and institutional needs. *Change, 30*(6), 18–25.

Marks, S. R. (1977). Multiple roles and role strain: Some notes on human energy, time, and commitment. *American Sociological Review, 42,* 921–936.

Mintzberg, H. (1973). *The nature of managerial work.* New York: Harper & Row.

Nippert-Eng, C. (1996). *Home and work.* Chicago: University of Chicago Press.

O'Driscoll, M. P., Ilgen, D. R., & Hildreth, K. (1992). Time devoted to job and off-job activities, inter-role conflict, and affective experiences. *Journal of Applied Psychology, 77,* 272–279.

Perna, L. W. (2001). The relationship between family responsibilities and employment status among college and university faculty. *Journal of Higher Education, 72*(5), 584–611.

Rapoport, R., Bailyn, L., Fletcher, J. K., & Pruitt, B. H. (2002). *Beyond work-family balance: Advancing gender equity and workplace performance.* San Francisco: Jossey Bass.

Rhoads, S. E., & Rhoads, C. H. (2003, July). *Gender roles and infant/toddler care: The special case of tenure track faculty.* Paper presented at the Association of American University Professors Symposium on Work/Family Issues, Washington, DC.

Robinson, J. P. (1997). *Time for life: The surprising ways Americans use their time.* University Park: Pennsylvania State University Press.

Roehling, P. V, Moen, P., & Batt, R. (2003). Spillover. In P. Moen (Ed), *It's about time: Couples and careers* (pp. 101–121). Ithaca, NY: Cornell University Press.

Sarbin, T. R., & Allen, V. L. (1968). Role theory. In G. Lindzey & E. Aronson (Eds.), *The handbook of social psychology* (Vol. 1, 2nd ed.). Reading, MA: Addison-Wesley.

Sax, L. J., Hagedorn, L. S., Marriscol, S., & DiCrisi, F. A., III. (2002). Faculty research productivity: Exploring the role of gender and family-related factors. *Research in Higher Education, 43*(4), 423–426.

Williams, J. (1999). *Unbending gender: Why family and work conflict and what to do about it.* New York: Oxford University Press.

Notes

1. All names are pseudonyms.

2. Because sleeping time consumed a substantial percentage of overall time, we elected to deduct sleeping hours and calculate percentages based on waking time from morning wake up until evening bedtime for each individual. We did, however, include the few minutes a couple of participants spent napping during the day as "personal needs and care." The amount of time participants reported sleeping varied from about four to nine hours per night, which was one contribution to differences in the total amount of time observed and reported for each participant. Another contribution to differences in total waking time across the participants was variation in the amount of time they recorded their home activities.

3

FACULTY WORK AND FAMILY LIFE

Policy Perspectives from Different Institutional Types

Lisa Wolf-Wendel and Kelly Ward

T he increasing number of women faculty of childbearing age in the academic workforce necessitates more proactive thinking about the policy context for faculty who seek to combine academic work with parenthood. Historically, academic institutions have foregone thinking about policies like parental leave and stopping the tenure clock (i.e., extending it) for childbirth because few faculty called for such policies. However, demographic shifts in the academic labor market have changed the landscape of the work and family policy arena. Contemporary college campuses have to deal forthrightly with policy issues surrounding work and family if they want to recruit and retain qualified faculty members, especially women with children (or those who want to have children).

Interest in research related to work and family in higher education has increased considerably over the past five years. This volume attests to such interest. The Sloan Foundation, in particular, has been supportive of the study of faculty work and family life and has funded numerous studies, including the one presented in this chapter. For the past three years we have been actively involved in a project looking at the experiences of women faculty who are new to the profession to see how they manage and integrate work and family in light of the demands of the tenure track.

Elsewhere we have looked at the experiences of tenure-track women at research universities to see how they manage academic life and parenthood

(Ward & Wolf-Wendel, 2004a), the fear women faculty with children face with regard to using work and family policies (Ward & Wolf-Wendel, 2004b), and the policy context of work and family at research universities (Wolf-Wendel & Ward, 2005). Thus far, a majority of our research, like much of the existing research on work and family, has focused on women at research universities. In this chapter we seek to expand this perspective to include not only findings from faculty at research universities but also faculty at other institutional types. This expansion is important as the majority of faculty work at other types of institutions (Hayes, 2003).

The focus of this chapter is the work/family policy context of different types of institutions. The focus on policy contexts includes examination of specific policies available for faculty who have children (e.g., parental leave) and also the general tenor of the campus when it comes to having children and being a parent. We wanted to know more about the availability of policies, their utility, and also the climate in which the policies are found and used.

Research Design

With the intent of learning more about the policy context and academic life in different institutional types from the perspective of junior[1] women faculty with young children, the following research questions guided this aspect of the study:

- What kinds of institutional policies are in existence to assist faculty members to balance work and family?
- How do these policies vary by institutional type?
- How are these policies perceived?
- How are work and family policies used and in what context?

To answer these questions, this study employs two sources of information. First, we interviewed women assistant professors who have children aged 0–5 years. The respondents came from research universities, comprehensive/regional institutions, liberal arts colleges, and community colleges. We interviewed about 30 women from each institutional type, for a total of 117 participants. The participants in the study represent a range of disciplinary backgrounds (hard sciences to the humanities to the professional schools) and represent variety in terms of geographic location and institutional prestige. (See Table 3.1 for a summary of the study participants.) The sample configuration supports the goal of the larger study: to learn more about how faculty members manage the dual roles of faculty and motherhood of young children within different institutional contexts. We also collected copies of the various institutional policies from each institution employing the women in the study. We conducted a content analysis of these policies, paying attention to differences and similarities within and across institutional types.

We identified study participants through existing networks, on-campus child care centers, and snowball sampling. Interviews lasted about 1.5 hours and were guided by a semistructured interview protocol. Questions focused on the relationship between professional life and parenthood, the presence and use of institutional policies, sources of support and tension, the tenure process, strategies for maintaining balance, and institutional and departmental context.

The transcribed interviews and the policies themselves were analyzed and interpreted using the constant comparative approach (Strauss & Corbin, 1990). We initially analyzed the data by looking for commonalities and differences within each institutional type. The data collection and analysis conform to the highest standards of qualitative research. Both researchers were involved in data collection and analysis, and were in constant communication about data collected and emerging themes. Our own position as professors and mothers provides additional perspective in collecting and analyzing the data. Member checks were conducted by selecting study participants to review and analyze working themes from the data to see if they resonated with individual experience. Feedback was then incorporated into the final

TABLE 3.1
Institutional and Departmental Characteristics of Sample

	Discipline			
Institutional Type	*Humanities*	*Social Sciences*	*Science, Math & Engineering*	*Professional Fields*
Community Colleges	11	5	8	7
Liberal Arts	13	8	5	5
Comprehensive	4	4	6	13
Research	5	4	11	8

narrative (Janesick, 2000). An audit trail was maintained through rigorous adherence to record keeping at all stages of data collection and analysis.

Findings

The purpose of this chapter is to look at how being a mother and a professor is experienced in light of various institutional policy contexts. When we talk about the policy context we are doing so inclusively. Interviews included questions about policies available for faculty having children (e.g., parental leave, stopping the tenure clock) and also about the larger campus environment and how it supports or inhibits family life (e.g., presence of day care facilities, how using policy is talked about).

The intent of the study is to learn how experiences take place in different institutional contexts, yet there are many commonalities across institutions. We address these first. With regard to policy, the findings from the study reveal that policies to support faculty as mothers are available to varying degrees. The Family Medical Leave Act (FMLA) was mentioned on all campuses and was the focal point of most institutional policies. The FMLA, by law, requires institutions to provide 12 weeks of unpaid leave (without jeopardizing one's job) for the birth of a child. At a minimum, campuses in the study were legally bound by FMLA and thus most mentioned the provisions of FMLA as an option for new mothers. Another commonality among the participants is that faculty felt they had to negotiate their own solutions to maternity-related needs (e.g., it was up to the women having the child to arrange with her unit head to take a leave, cover her classes, stop the tenure clock, etc.). The existence of institutional policies to support these women was not a major factor in determining their course of action in either having a baby or using policies. Generally speaking, the onus to negotiate work and family was placed on the faculty member herself and there was the general perception that campuses were not particularly helpful to women faculty having children.

Further, in terms of the climate aspect of the policy context, we found that the mere presence of a policy does not mean that faculty will feel the freedom to use the available options. This supports existing research on this topic that addresses the culture of the workplace and how it can facilitate or inhibit the use of policies that are in place (Hochschild, 1997; Tierney & Bensimon, 1996). How this is manifest varies by campus, but the actual presence of fear and concern about policy usage was common across faculty members at all institutional types. We have written about this concern more fully in an article in *Academe* (Ward & Wolf-Wendel, 2004b). Other work and family researchers have also addressed this issue (e.g., Drago & Colbeck, 2003; Finkel, Olswang, & She, 1994). There was universal concern about how using policies like parental leave would be perceived by colleagues and the ultimate effect taking a leave would have on tenure decisions. In fact, of the 37 women who could have stopped the tenure clock (because such policies existed on their campus), only 9 (24%) opted to do so.

We found the experience of being an academic and a mother is one that shares significant commonality across campuses. The focus here, however, is to tease out the different nuances that exist on campuses with regard to the work and family policy context. We now turn to the findings that are distinct for each campus type included in the study.

Research Universities

The content analysis of the policy documents at the 10 research universities included in the study reveal that FMLA is universally mentioned as the primary policy vehicle that allows for maternity leave. In addition, a majority of the research universities had policies that noted the option to request stopping the tenure clock in the event of the birth of a child. Only one campus in the study offered paid leave that was separate from sick or disability leave. Based on the limited availability of paid leave, we were not surprised that a majority of the research university faculty in the study did not use any type of leave and, in fact, went to great lengths to avoid using leave.

Data analysis reveals that most of the women in the study did not even know what policies were available nor was this information made readily available. As one respondent indicated, "I was the first person in my department at [campus] to have a child in nineteen years . . . and that is why there was such an open interpretation of the maternity leave policy." Such comments were quite typical among the research university respondents.

Even though some women "didn't even know the regulations for maternity leave and how much time you get, or how that works," others used maternity leave policies and tenure-clock stops when they had their children. For these women, the use of policy was a mixed blessing. On the one hand, women found "turning back the tenure clock definitely made a difference" on the other hand, there was concern that using the policy "would make me look less serious" or "hurt me somehow." In short, those who took leave did so with trepidation and those who did not take leave did so to avoid bias and potential repercussion. Regardless, fear was a driving force behind women's decisions about taking leave. This confirms other research on the policy context of research universities and how it affects faculty decisions about taking parental leave (e.g., Drago & Colbeck, 2003; Finkel, Olswang, & She, 1994; Hochschild, 1997; Raabe, 1997; Ward & Wolf-Wendel, 2004a; Ward & Wolf-Wendel, 2004b).

On the positive side, a few of the faculty members we interviewed were in departments with greater than average levels of communication and support. In these rare cases, stopping the clock for childbirth was viewed positively. As noted by one professor: "My department chair mentioned it [stopping the clock] to me because of pregnancy; she saw where I was in my career and thought it would be a bad idea for me not to take a leave and stop the clock." This same professor went on to say, "I obviously want to get tenure and I have to stay here, but I wasn't one of those people who wanted to get it as fast as I can. . . . It's a natural step whether I get it in five years or ten years." This quote points to the crucial role department chairs play in helping faculty decide to take a leave and helping them make the necessary arrangements.

The preoccupation with the decision to take parental leave (or not) had two dimensions: (1) logistics and how to arrange a leave, given that the typical semester is 15 weeks and most leaves are between 6 and 12 weeks and (2) perceptions of colleagues and how they would think about a person's absence (this was particularly the case for faculty who were in the first or second year of their positions). In contrast, the decision to stop the tenure clock had more to do with concern about what long-term effect it would have on one's career. Officially (and legally) the time one has off as part of an official stopped clock (regardless of reason) is not supposed to count as part of a faculty member's dossier when she does go up for tenure. In practice, however, it is hard to implement and also harder to document how it does affect someone's tenure bid. One faculty member eloquently spoke to this issue:

> Statutorily you are supposed to be able to stop the tenure clock when you have kids. However, I don't think any slack is being cut based on you having kids. I personally feel like expectations here are very high. You can take the time you need to be with your kids as long it doesn't interfere with

your output at all. It is sort of your time management problem—if you want to take three months off to stay at home with your baby that's fine but down the road, you can't say "I spent time with my kids and I only published four papers."

Officially this faculty member, like others in the study, had taken a leave and slowed or otherwise stopped the tenure clock; however, it was not without repercussion or at least the fear and threat of it.

Outsider reviewers play a particularly important role in the evaluation of tenure-track faculty in research universities. At top-tier institutions, in particular, faculty are expected to be nationally known in their field to earn tenure, and the external review process is in place to contribute to assessment of the emerging role as expert. Leave policies not only need to be communicated internally, they must also be communicated externally to reviewers. One respondent noted, "People writing letters nationally, which here is the biggest weight, don't cut any slack." Another faculty noted that external reviewers are likely to note a gap in productivity and are not interested in why the gap occurred.

In sum, the predominant finding for faculty at research universities was the pressing concern about what impact using leave policies would have on research productivity and ultimately tenure decisions. Faculty wanted to avoid being perceived of as needy while on the tenure track. Fear emanating from using policies related to parenthood was a prevalent theme throughout the interviews at all institutions, but the focus on how this fear would affect tenure was most pronounced at research universities. There was a general preoccupation with how using leave would be viewed by colleagues and department chairs, and germane to the topic of research universities, how it would figure into the tenure decision.

Comprehensive Colleges and Universities

As an institutional category, comprehensive colleges and universities are a diverse group of institutions, with some more focused on gaining a national reputation and others more regionally focused (Clark, 1987). When viewed from a policy perspective, however, we found that the concerns of faculty with young children were fairly consistent regardless of the focus and mission of the institution within this institutional type. Faculty at comprehensive colleges and universities, like those at research universities, also had concerns with how having a baby would affect the tenure decision and the faculty career as a whole. The predominant theme in the interviews at the comprehensives, however, had to do with the extremely informal nature of the policy context, which left the women we interviewed feeling unsure of what policies were even available and how to go about using them if they were available.

The content analysis of the policy documents from the comprehensives in the study shows that the majority of the campuses in the study offered only the provisions provided by the FMLA. Only one of the 17 campuses mentioned stopping the tenure clock specifically for the birth of a child and only one offered paid leave. Generally, the comprehensive institutions in our sample were not very progressive on the work and family policy front.

The informal atmosphere with regard to work and family is a likely outgrowth of the limited availability of policies. We were initially surprised by the number of faculty who simply did not know what family-related policies were available—the assumption was that no policies were available and that any existing policies would not be useful. Further examination of the policies shows that these assumptions were grounded. What this meant for the women in the study was the need to organize one's own maternity leave and to work with the department chair in doing so. On these campuses, department chairs played a pivotal role in helping study participants figure out how to make taking a leave work within the strictures of the semester schedule. This typically meant department chairs agreeing to or fine-tuning plans that the women faculty themselves came up with in working out the logistics of a parental leave.

In contrast to faculty at research universities, where the main preoccupation with leave and tenure revolved around research, the preoccupation for faculty at comprehensive colleges was with arranging course schedules in relation to a leave. Given the informal policy situation, most departments had no methodical way of covering classes in the event of an extended absence (e.g., a 12-week parental leave). Of all the interviews we conducted, only one faculty member mentioned that the department chair simply took care of hiring an adjunct to cover classes while she took a six-week leave when her baby was born. Other faculty spoke of "asking friends to cover classes," "only teaching on Wednesdays so I wasn't away from the baby much," "[my] TA [covering] the last two weeks of the semester after the baby was born," and "banking courses until next semester." These were all devices faculty used to cover courses since adjuncts were generally unavailable. Again, with a semester schedule it can be very difficult to figure out how to take a 6- to 12-week leave when typical semesters are 15 weeks long.

In addition to the challenge of handling logistics for sometimes as many as four classes a semester, faculty mentioned how awkward it was to have to make such arrangements with colleagues to cover classes, as one describes in the following:

> It's really yucky [to ask people to cover classes] because they don't like to hire people [i.e., adjuncts] here. What ends up happening is that you have to ask your fellow colleagues. Here, they are all wonderful and I was lucky and did it happily. But, I just think it is a horrible position to put someone in if they don't have as good of a group around as I did.

Faculty new to the institution and also having a baby found this situation to be particularly awkward because in addition to the stress of being new and untenured, they had to worry about how to cover their classes once they had a baby. These women were in vulnerable situations and often didn't know the culture of the institution enough to determine an acceptable or reasonable accommodation. A faculty member who had a baby in the first semester of a new faculty job talked about it this way:

> I asked about maternity leave and was told there is no maternity leave here, there is no policy for it and what faculty women do is take sick leave, but you can't do that because you have to be employed at least 6 months before you can take sick leave or disability. And, of course, there was no sick leave accrued anyway [since I was new]. . . . I didn't really think that much about just going along with the flow and they did give me a course reduction for that first semester from three to two so I was teaching two new courses for me, one at the doctoral level and one master's. I started right in when the semester started and then three weeks later, on September 22, I had the baby. I had the baby on Friday and so I had my classes that week on Tuesday and Wednesday online and then I was back in the classroom the next week.

This professor went on to say, "I must have been crazy" and "now I'm a little resentful that no one even mentioned taking time off." This is not to say that people were not kind to her and to others having children, as babies tend to bring out kindnesses in people. What it does say, however, is that the policy environments at these comprehensive colleges were ill equipped to handle the basic needs of faculty as new mothers.

The focus for faculty at comprehensive institutions was on how having a baby would work around teaching schedules and, further, on taking parental leave. There was little mention of stopping the tenure clock and of how having a baby would affect research productivity. In general, faculty felt that their institutions were open to them taking time off, but the time off would be without pay (which few could afford) and arranging course schedules and replacements was up to the faculty member taking the leave, not the institution or its representatives. This meant that for some, taking leave was not worth the hassle, negotiation, and potential repercussions.

Liberal Arts Colleges

The content analysis of the policy statements reveals that the liberal arts colleges are generally the most progressive institutional type when it comes to parental leave policies. These campuses offered the most in terms of policy options. Of the 13 liberal arts campuses included in the study, 6 offer some type of provision for paid leave. While all liberal arts college campuses mention FMLA, a majority of them went beyond the minimum required by law. In general, the more selective liberal arts colleges in the study were more progressive in their policies; we surmise that this is a function of greater campus financial health and therefore the ability to pay for more comprehensive policies.

The predominant finding from the women we interviewed at liberal arts colleges is that the family orientation of these colleges does help shape a more family-friendly environment in terms of policy. Like women at other colleges, for those who did not take a semester-length leave quite a bit of negotiating still had to take place in terms of how to arrange for covering missed classes and the like. But, haggling with department chairs was not a predominant theme as it was at the comprehensive colleges. Given the more highly evolved nature of the policy environment, the interview comments about policy were not so much focused on how to cover classes when having a baby as they were concerned with things like adding adoption to the leave policies and changing times for faculty meetings to be more family friendly. Once more basic needs are met, faculty can and do focus on those needs that are more advanced.

The contrast of the liberal arts college campuses with policies to campuses without strong policies is stark. A faculty member from a liberal arts campus without a policy that goes beyond FMLA had this to say: "I was up on my feet and teaching in front of the classroom the first day of classes, which was 10 days after a C-section. I was two weeks into the semester where I remember thinking 'I had made the biggest mistake that I had ever made in my life.'" This faculty member works in a policy environment that did not provide any type of paid leave and she could not afford to take an unpaid leave. Her experience stands in contrast to another faculty member in our sample who had modified duties in the semester after she had a baby, which meant she "took a half time parent leave at full salary yet taught only one course." The half-time parental leave offered by her campus allows faculty members to either take off the semester they have a baby for 50% of salary or to work a modified load (which is roughly half-time) for full salary. Such a leave led this faculty member to say "I had no problem at [my campus]"—a statement that was unique among those offered by the women in the study regardless of institutional type. In short, on campuses where leave must be negotiated there is a preoccupation with how to cover classes and other responsibilities with the onus on the faculty member to do the arranging. In contrast, on campuses with formal leave policies, the process of negotiating and figuring out how to cover faculty responsibilities tends to rest on the department chair.

The general tenor of the interview findings from the faculty at the liberal arts colleges was more focused on children and family in general, than on birth and babies. We interpret this to mean that when institutions have more progressive policies, women feel less threatened about the viability of their jobs when they decide to have a baby, which allows them to be concerned about things like campuswide faculty meetings at 4:30 that "always run over creating a real problem for day care pick up." Further, there was concern about things like coordinating the college's schedule with the local school district or providing affordable, accessible child care—again, issues that have more to do with families in general than with having a baby.

Other findings from the liberal arts college faculty related to policy had to do with campus culture and campus expectations for women who have children while working at a liberal arts college. Two expectations were prevalent: (1) that a woman having a baby will do so in May to save the campus from having to deal with leave (whether paid or unpaid) and (2) that a woman will have only one baby while on the tenure track. The preoccupation with pregnancy timing is not necessarily unique to liberal arts college faculty (timing was a preoccupation of nearly everyone in the study), but this was the only institutional type in which women faculty suggested that it was the culture of the campus that encouraged women to time the arrival of their babies in May. As one faculty member explained, "Faculty are expected to have children in May, thus allowing them to take the summer off to avoid time off for maternity leave and then to just come back in the Fall." While this faculty member did have her baby in May, she told us it was not planned, "it just worked out that way." This professor noted that her colleagues and department chair complimented her on her timing.

The expectation and campus lore about having only one baby was also expressed as a part of the culture at many liberal arts colleges. We found, for example, that on campuses with paid leaves it was easy to use the leave policy for baby number one but more difficult to use the policy for subsequent pregnancies. Faculty members thinking about having a second baby while on the tenure track, did so with trepidation about how it would be viewed to stop the tenure clock twice and to take two leaves. We learned from the interviews that faculty felt that one baby is tolerated, but having two might just push one's luck to the limit. One faculty member relayed a conversation she had with her department chair about taking a second leave: "She [my department chair] said it was unprecedented to ask for two [maternity leaves and clock delays]. People haven't had two kids pre-tenure before." Ultimately, this faculty member got a new chair who granted a second leave without fanfare, but the point remains that the policy environment does shape a woman's decision to have a child, when to have it, and how many to have.

Community Colleges

Most of the community colleges in the sample listed the FMLA as the only policy relevant to helping employees who are seeking assistance related to work and family. Though all community colleges are covered under FMLA, only 12 of the 18 colleges in the sample listed any type of parent-related policies. None of the community colleges mentioned paid maternity leave policies, though some indicated that women may use sick leave or disability leave for maternity purposes. Only one institution listed anything other than FMLA or sick leave, offering a provision to allow probationary faculty to stop the tenure clock for childbirth.

Faculty at community colleges experience fairly controlled environments when it comes to work and therefore family. The faculty we interviewed painted a picture of the community college work environment as one that does not allow for much flexibility and autonomy because of the demands of heavy course loads and required office hours. Community college faculty members in the study were required to teach between 24 and 32 credit hours or their equivalent per contract year. Most were required to be on campus a minimum of 35 hours per week, including teaching, office hours, advising, and providing service to the department and institution. The birth of a child required faculty members to figure out how to cover their classes during the semester in which they had a child; this was a concern for the 11 women in our community college sample who had their children while in the probationary period. The other women in the sample had their children before beginning their full-time employment as faculty and thus were less concerned about maternity leave policies and more concerned about the general climate of the campus as it pertained to balancing work and family.

It is important to note that the probationary period for full-time community college faculty is typically three years, and that professors are granted tenure based primarily on their classroom performance. Earning tenure was typically not an area of intense concern for the faculty we interviewed, as most believed that they were good teachers and would be granted tenure as a matter of due course. Nonetheless, some of the women did express trepidation about the effect that having a baby might have on their eventually earning tenure. As one faculty member explained, "You know, even with my feeling fairly confident about the tenure system here . . . I do wonder if I should just make sure I get the tenure first and then have the other baby." Another faculty member advised new colleagues to "wait until they're not probationary [to have a baby] because I could see how [maternity leave arrangements] could come back and slap them in the face."

When asked about the maternity-related policies on their campus, half of the participants mentioned the options of using sick leave, catastrophic illness leave, or disability leave, and about half indicated that the option open to them was unpaid leave through FMLA. Some faculty also mentioned that they understood that it was best to time the arrival of children for summer or semester break as there was no workable institutional policy for them to use. On the more progressive end of the spectrum, several women said that they were offered a reduced teaching load, they worked with colleagues or department chairs to cover their classes in their absence, they taught online courses that allowed more flexibility to accommodate the birth of their child, or they negotiated arrangements with their chair that made taking a leave unnecessary.

The use of sick leave in lieu of maternity leave was perceived to be problematic for faculty at community colleges. Most of the women were less worried about the tenure implications of using sick leave than they were about the negative implications of using their sick leave as parental leave. They worried about what would happen during subsequent illnesses of the child or themselves. Further, they did not like the association of parental leave with sick leave or catastrophic illness because of the negative connotations. One woman expressed these concerns accordingly: "They make you use up all your sick leave . . . so when you are done having a child, you have no sick leave and that's very hard because . . . I have to use sick leave to take him to the doctor. The fact that they bundle you into a medical emergency just like somebody who broke a leg or had a heart attack or something is awful."

The use of any kind of leave from teaching was a concern for many of the faculty members. They suggested that while the leave (either unpaid or sick) was offered, there was this subtle implication that you ought not to use it. One professor explained, "I feel a sense of support from my department . . . everyone has been very supportive and very generous and has been really excited about the pregnancy and about the baby . . . but I do kind of feel as if there's this underlying tension about making certain I hold up my end of the bargain." Still another professor told us that when she approached her division chair about going on maternity leave he said, "You can go on leave, but please don't take it." And a third professor who used sick leave for maternity leave told us that her dean asked, "When are you coming back?" It was very much this business thing: "What kind of burden are you putting on me and the department?"

Interestingly, while most of the campuses were unionized, very few of the faculty members talked about the role of faculty unions in addressing work/family concerns, let alone mentioning the union's role in advocating for such policies. One faculty member suggested that the union was more concerned with salary than with quality-of-life issues. Still, given the presence of faculty unions on these campuses we were somewhat surprised about the ad hoc nature of maternity-related accommodations. It appeared that some departments and division heads were sympathetic and accommodating, while others created an extremely hostile work environment. The most extreme case was a woman whose department chair created a building policy barring children (for "liability reasons"); this chair also told this faculty member that she could not use a breast pump in the building or bring a cooler to the office to store breast milk, as that would "make this building appear to be a cafeteria." A more helpful department chair told his new faculty member that instead of taking a leave she ought to teach her courses online. The faculty member was told, "I don't know how I would feel about an adjunct walking in week 8 of the semester and taking over. What about we do this deal: you stay home and still do them [online courses] and I won't take as much sick leave out of your pay." The professor figured she didn't have any other options and that this was a workable, though difficult, solution given the workload associated with online classes.

Beyond the need for maternity leave, faculty at community colleges expressed the need for policies related to both child care and support for breast-feeding mothers. The faculty were unanimous in their request for affordable child care on campus that was available to faculty members. Some added that it would be helpful for the institution to offer child care allowances for faculty, child care visitation, and extended child care hours. The need for support for breast-feeding mothers seemed a unique concern among community college faculty—a concern that stems from the fact that many of the faculty members didn't have their own offices. Finding a private place to use one's breast pump was a concern for many of the women we interviewed. Most made do on their own with this issue—pumping in the restroom or making arrangements with office mates. One woman discovered that OSHA requires workplaces to provide pumping rooms and requested that her dean comply. Another woman describes how her colleagues made a sign with a picture of nursing puppies on it that said: "New mother inside. Please knock." Another stated: "I pumped in my office . . . my office mate was sympathetic but it was still inconvenient. I had to think of putting a post-it on the door before I did it. You know, you can hear the noises in the hallway, while I have my boobs exposed at my desk, the pumping machine going, I hoped she saw the post-it before she came in after class." Another faculty member was told that she shouldn't store her breast milk in the department refrigerator because someone might mistake it for creamer. Each of these women wanted some space, acceptance for their decision to breast-feed, and acknowledgment that this was a necessary accommodation that should be easy to fulfill and ought to be a nonissue.

Analysis, Conclusions, Implications

The findings from this research project suggest a rather tenuous policy environment with regard to work and family at all institutional types. We found that mothers of young children have two different types of policy needs: (1) concerns related to the birth of a child, including the need for maternity leave or the need to stop the tenure clock; and (2) needs related to being a parent in the long term, including access to child care and concerns about scheduling classes and meetings. Most institutions focus their policies, however inadequate they may be, on the first set of needs. Only a handful of campuses extend their policies to respond to the second set of needs.

This study also shows that while the advent of FMLA legislation had done great things to put the need for work and family policies on the conscience of contemporary society, it has also absolved institutions of their responsibility to translate policy to the unique needs of faculty. However, we also found that some campuses were not even in full compliance with FMLA. Campus policies and FMLA language tend to exist on campuses simultaneously, but there is limited translation between the two. For example, it is common for campuses to have language that allows for a 6-week unpaid leave in the event of the birth of a child whereas FMLA allows for 12. This leaves faculty to ask, how much leave am I entitled to? The length of leave time allowed in FMLA is also problematic as it does not coincide with a typical semester length—thus requiring someone (either the faculty member or a departmental representative) to figure out how to deliver entire courses. Clearly, the findings from our study suggest that FMLA alone is not enough.

Further, FMLA makes no provision for any paid leave and campuses, in general, have not been very progressive in providing paid leave for faculty having children. Few new faculty members are in a position to be able to afford a semester without pay. Thus, if a faculty member wants to take a paid leave, in most circumstances, she must use sick leave. This assumes that faculty members have accrued sufficient sick leave, which for new faculty members may not be the case. It also assumes that pregnancy is a sickness, which is problematic because it equates pregnancy and childbirth with pathology. Further, asking faculty members to use sick leave creates a dilemma if and when a faculty member and/or a family member actually becomes ill—as their sick leave will surely be depleted.

Aside from the problems rooted in the types and source of leaves available, there was also the fear expressed by faculty members in our study about using leaves or stopping the tenure clock. While some women took advantage of these policies, they did so fearing both the short-term and long-term repercussions. Those at research universities worried about the effect of taking a leave on their research productivity as well as perceptions of colleagues about their commitment to scholarship. Those at the other institutional types worried about how to cover their classes and about how colleagues would perceive their choices. As a result of this fear, many women faculty members decided not to use any leave, even if it was potentially available to them.

Equally problematic is the fact that the women in our study were the primary agents of action responsible for negotiating their own accommodations. They were responsible for coming up with a plan for how to cover classes during a leave and then had to approach their department chair for approval to carry out the plan. Faculty members should bear some responsibility for negotiating solutions to their concerns, but they deserve to be supported in this process. Ideally, department chairs will not only be open to suggestions on ways to address the needs of their faculty members, but will be prepared and willing to proactively offer solutions to their faculty members who are pregnant. New professors are in a vulnerable position, they are worried about how they are perceived by their senior colleagues and they need guidance through the process of negotiating the use and application of family-related policies. Failure to provide such guidance will create a situation where women don't use policies that are available to them or fail to negotiate solutions that serve them well.

Recommendations

The findings from this study suggest that the policy environment regarding work and family can be improved. How to improve it, however, is something that often stymies faculty and administrators. The findings also suggest that the primary onus for making the policies that are available work is on the faculty member herself. Clearly, the faculty member in need of leave to help manage childbirth has an active role in using policy. However, the faculty member can only be successful in using policies if those policies are available and open to use. The findings from this study point to the general need for a more highly evolved policy environment in higher education regarding faculty, work, and family. Based on the findings of our research we offer the following policy recommendations:

- Go beyond FMLA, offer leave and release-time options that are more focused on meeting the needs of faculty who are having children.

  The creation and implementation of the FMLA has helped put the concerns of families on the policy map in higher education and other sectors of work and in this way has been invaluable to work and family policy in general. However, the FMLA is only a start; it is not a policy end in itself, yet many campuses use it that way. Campus policy makers need to look closely at the FMLA and what it provides and then fill in missing gaps.
- Provide paid leaves that are separate from sick leave or disability leave.

  By relying on sick or disability leave as the primary vehicle for faculty to take paid leave, campuses juxtapose pregnancy and childbirth with sickness. This is problematic on two fronts: (1) pregnancy is not a sickness, and (2) if sickness of parent or child does occur there is limited availability of leave to use sick leave as it is intended—for sickness. We recognize that offering paid leave for faculty to cover childbirth and recuperation is an expensive proposition. Yet offering such a provision to faculty communicates that campuses value faculty and that pregnancy is distinct from sickness.
- Consider modified-duty policies.

  The findings from our research suggest that faculty sometimes don't feel that they need a full leave to accommodate having a child. Modified duties can provide a win-win situation for faculty and the institutions where they work. Typically faculty with modified duties get full pay, but have some type of reduction or reorganization of workload. For example, if a faculty member has a child in September, for the fall semester she may only teach one course instead of two, limit involvement in service obligations, and maintain involvement in research though forego involvement in conferences. Modified duty might also call for faculty to serve in some type of administrative capacity or to engage in a project for the department in lieu of other types of work obligations. Such options keep the faculty member on campus (and therefore can quell fears about being out of sight and out of mind) and keeps them active in their work, albeit in a limited way. The modified-duties approach recognizes the rhythms of the faculty career in which some times are more productive than others. Most institutions grant faculty the ebb and flow of the faculty career. A modified-duties policy recognizes that these ebbs and flows can happen concurrent with childbirth.

- Provide tenure clock extensions and communicate their use.

Stopping the tenure clock is one of the most common ways that institutions accommodate junior faculty who face circumstances such as childbirth that can cause a temporary setback in productivity (Sullivan, Hollenshead, & Smith, 2004). Unfortunately, the findings from our research (and other research as well) suggest that faculty do not feel free to stop their tenure clock for fear of repercussion. Campuses need to not only *provide* the opportunity to stop the clock, they also need to let faculty know it is "safe" to *use* such a policy. Policy makers need to provide clear directions on how the policy can be used and be clear not only with the faculty member using the policy, but more important, with those who will judge her productivity come review time on how a tenure extension will be evaluated. It can be useful to provide examples and scenarios so faculty can see how an extension can work as part of a successful tenure process.

- Develop a list of possible accommodations for faculty to use in relation to family leave and communicate those to department chairs and faculty members.

Many campuses are quite creative in how they accommodate faculty who have children while on the tenure track, yet many of these accommodations are negotiated informally and privately. We recommend that campuses provide lots of examples of how faculty might manage having a child while maintaining their career. By providing examples, policy makers can show faculty members, their department chairs, and their colleagues possible scenarios for taking a leave, given the timing of the birth and the stage of career.

- Educate deans and department chairs about the range of options and policies available. Make sure that they communicate this to their faculty.

Our research indicates that too often the first time a department chair thinks about parental leave is when a woman faculty member knocks on the door with news of a pregnancy, leaving the department chair off guard and uncertain how to best accommodate the faculty member. Work and family needs to be part of dean and department chair orientation, administrative handbooks, and ongoing training. Administrators need to know what policies are available and be aware of how policies can best be used. Further, these administrators need to educate their faculties about how to best accommodate the pregnancy of a colleague. This latter recommendation may seem like common sense, but the findings from our research suggest that it is colleagues who are often the most insensitive about work and family concerns.

- In addition to dealing with the immediate needs of faculty having babies, attend to the more long-term concerns by supporting parents with children.

Dealing with faculty when they have a baby is only the first step to helping faculty manage work and family concerns. Family needs are ongoing. Across the board in our study we learned that finding affordable and accessible day care was a major challenge for faculty with children. While it may not be realistic that all campuses provide day care centers to meet the needs of faculty, campuses would do well to identify and make available day care services. These types of policies can also involve creating teaching and meeting schedules that allow parents to work with day care centers and local schools.

- Last, it is important for all campuses to recognize that faculty, men and women, young and old, have lives outside of work.

The focus of this chapter is creating policy (and campus environments in general) that more fully support the combination of work and family for faculty. Such an approach is not just about faculty with families. Faculty members of all ages, genders, and work stages have lives that extend beyond the workplace, whether it is related to family or not. Too often the academic workplace is consuming and geared toward a work ethic that thrives on constant work (read workaholism). Needless to say, such an approach is not healthy for any faculty member and certainly not those with young families. Policy makers need to recognize faculty as whole people with divergent interests and demands that go beyond the workplace. Creating a campus culture that allows faculty to combine work and family is good for everyone; it will enhance faculty recruitment and retention, lead to higher faculty morale, and it will, in the end, be good for the institution as well as its faculty.

References

Clark, B. R. (1987). *The academic life: Small worlds, different worlds.* Princeton, NJ: Carnegie Foundation for the Advancement of Teaching.

Drago, R., & Colbeck, C. (2003). *Final report from the mapping project: Exploring the terrain of U.S. colleges and universities for faculty and families.* University Park: Pennsylvania State University.

Finkel, S. K., Olswang, S., & She, N. (1994). Childbirth, tenure, and promotion for women faculty. *Review of Higher Education, 17*(3), 259–270.

Hayes, W. (2003). *So you want to be a college professor?* Lanham, MD: Scarecrow Press.

Hochschild, A. R. (1997). *The time bind: When work becomes home and home becomes work.* New York: Henry Holt.

Janesick, V. J. (2000). The choreography of qualitative research design: Minuets, improvisations, and crystallization. In N. K. Denzin & Y. S. Lincoln (Eds.), *Handbook of qualitative research* (pp. 379–400). Thousand Oaks, CA: Sage.

Raabe, P. H. (1997). Work-family policies for faculty: How "career-and-family-friendly" is academe? In M. A. Ferber & J. W. Loeb (Eds.), *Academic couples: Problems and promises* (pp. 208–225). Urbana: University of Illinois Press.

Strauss, A., & Corbin, J. (1990). Basics of qualitative research: Grounded theory procedures and techniques. Newbury Park, CA: Sage.

Sullivan, B., Hollenshead, C. S., & Smith, G. (2004). Developing and implementing work-family policies for faculty. *Academe, 90*(6), 24–27.

Tierney, W. G., & Bensimon, E. M. (1996). *Promotion and tenure: Community and socialization in academe.* Albany, NY: SUNY Press.

Ward, K., & Wolf-Wendel, L. E. (2004a). Academic motherhood: Managing complex roles in research universities. *Review of Higher Education, 27*(2), 233–257.

Ward, K., & Wolf-Wendel, L. E. (2004b). Fear factor: How safe is it to make time for family? *Academe, 90*(6), 28–31.

Wolf-Wendel, L., & Ward, K. (2005). Policy contexts for work and family: Perspectives from research university faculty. In Curtis, J. (Ed.), *The challenge of balancing faculty careers and family work. New Directions for Higher Education* (p. 130). San Francisco: Jossey-Bass.

Notes

1. Junior women faculty include those not yet tenured at institutions with a tenure system and within the first three years for institutions that use contract systems.

4

POLICIES THAT PART

Early Career Experiences of Coworking Academic Couples

Elizabeth G. Creamer

T here is little systematic research about the impact of work/life policies on faculty lives. This chapter examines the early career experiences of nine coworking academic couples. Their retrospective
accounts provide insight about their initial attraction and the compacts they
made during the decision to enter a long-term relationship. The strategies
couples deployed to establish their intellectual autonomy often jeopardized
their commitment to "keep it equal." To create a culture that is family
friendly requires examination of the values communicated by all policies and
practices that have a significant impact on faculty lives, including those involving reward and recognition.

It is the habit of Western thought to envision creativity as arising from
individual insight. "Creativity begins in a single mind," Fox and Faver wrote
in 1984. This ideological assumption is reflected in the emphasis placed on
individual accomplishments in the traditional academic reward structure.
Social constructionists see knowledge production in an entirely different
way. From this theoretical perspective, knowledge is constructed through dialogue and shaped by powerful contextual forces, including intellectual perspectives of the time and other dynamics of the environment and personal

I presented earlier versions of this chapter, first at the 2003 annual meeting of the Association for the
Study of Higher Education (ASHE) in Sacramento, California, and later at the 2004 American Association for Higher Education (AAHE) annual meeting in San Diego, California.

relationships (John-Steiner, 1997, 2000). This perspective considers interaction as central to creativity and knowledge production.

The individualistic values that are the center of the traditional academic reward structure offer one explanation why early-career faculty often voice a concern about a sense of isolation and lack of community (Trower, Austin, & Sorcinelli, 2001). "Scholars in their early years on the job reported experiencing loneliness, isolation, competition, and sometimes incivility" (p. 5). Given this context and that they have yet to develop the collegial networks that will sustain them through midcareer and late career, it is not surprising that early-career faculty may turn to someone they trust, such as a domestic partner, as they try to carve out a niche for themselves in the profession and learn the ropes of teaching and research.

Dual-career academic couples have been a sizable presence on college campuses for decades (Loeb, 2001). Thirty-five percent of male academics and 40% of female academics have a spouse or partner who is also employed in higher education (Astin & Milem, 1997). Detailed information about how many full-time, tenure-track faculty have a spouse in a comparable position is hard to find, but evidence suggests the percentage is quite modest. Faculty women in fields where they are underrepresented, most notably engineering and science, are significantly more likely than their male counterparts to have a partner who is a college or university professor (Fox, 2004). Spousal hiring policies are strongly linked to recruiting women faculty in science and engineering.

Coworking couples—defined as those who merge their public and private lives by sharing work-related tasks—are a small subset of dual-career couples. Scholarly collaboration among academic couples is not unusual. A study of sociologists married to other professional sociologists found that 30% had jointly authored a book and almost half had published one or more jointly authored articles (Goodman, Royce, Selvin, & Weinstein, 1984). Thirty percent of the respondents to a questionnaire I distributed to senior faculty at research universities had coauthored a book or journal articles, and 60% reported that they exchanged feedback with a spouse about draft manuscripts (Creamer & Associates, 2001, appendix B). That the majority of respondents had exchanged feedback about manuscripts points to a form of invisible or unacknowledged labor that influences productivity. The contribution of invisible labor provided by family members, particularly a spouse, to scientific and artistic insight has been documented by a number of authors

(Perry & Brownley, 1984; Rose, 1994). Sharing credit for authorship is one way collaborators make visible the intellectual contribution of a partner.

This chapter examines the early-career experiences of 9 coworking academic couples.[1] I use the retrospective accounts provided by coworking couples who are now senior academics at research universities to describe the personal and intellectual foundation of their initial attraction, the compacts they made during the decision to marry or enter a long-term relationship, and how they responded to the injunctions of academic reward structure. The accommodations couples made to the demands of the academic reward structure illustrate the central thesis of this chapter, which is that how institutions interpret and implement promotion and tenure policies is one of many reflections of a couple-friendly and family-friendly culture.

In 1997 and 1998, I interviewed both members of 9 couples in all but 1 case, for a total of 17 interviews. The couples are almost equally divided between those entering faculty careers in the early to mid-1970s and the early to mid-1980s. These couples are unusual in that all but 1 pair held comparable, senior-level, tenure-track faculty positions at the same institution. Participants provided me with a copy of their curriculum vita, which included a detailed account of their publications. While largely in the social sciences, participants had backgrounds in a variety of academic disciplines including geology, geography, sociology, psychology, special education, anthropology, and communication studies. None of the couples is located at the same research university. Four of the 9 couples have children. All but 2 of the couples can be described as career-equal or career symmetrical and 4 have records that show such strong symmetry that it cannot be coincidental. Significant differences in career age or stage characterize two relationships.

Related Literature

There has been little systematic research that documents the impact of work/life policies on faculty work and personal lives (Norrell & Norrell, 1996). Publications that exist are often largely anecdotal (see, for example, Smart & Smart, 1990; Bird & Bird, 1987). Sociologists have been at the forefront of research about dual-career academic couples where academic couples figure prominently in studies about egalitarian family forms (e.g., Hochschild, 1997; Risman, 1998; Schwartz, 1994). These maintain a one-way focus on the impact of work on home and family life by defining egalitarianism, not in terms of the priority of work as Scanzoni and Scanzoni (1976) proposed, but in terms of the division of labor on household matters. I have argued elsewhere (Creamer & Associates, 2001) that another way to frame the discussion about work/family issues is to reverse the formula. Rather than examining how the demands of work drive daily family life and the division of labor in the household, as Arlie Hochschild has done so remarkably, I believe we should examine how family life is shaped to affect productivity, as is done through coworking.

Evidence exists in the research literature that a partner in the same profession has a positive impact on faculty research productivity, as measured by publication counts. The major conclusion of a cross-sectional analysis of four national databases produced between 1969 and 1993 is that men and women benefit *equally* from the human capital of a highly educated spouse (Xie & Shauman, 1998). Xie and Shauman conclude that the prime benefit of marriage is not relief from domestic responsibilities, but from the "high human capital of their spouses, who tend to be highly educated professionals" (p. 860). This means that ready access to the skills and expertise of a highly trained professional is instrumental to enhancing the productivity of the member of a dual-career academic couple.

The failure to find significant differences between men's and women's research productivity when structural factors are controlled, such as institutional location and position (Xie & Shauman, 1998), has led to the speculation that egalitarian family forms explain how married women manage to remain as productive, if not more productive, than their single counterparts. Hochschild, the author of *The Time Bind* (1997), labeled egalitarianism as a "contingent" phenomenon, driven more by the demands of full-time work than by ideological commitment. She wrote, rather acerbically,

> This study demonstrates that these lifestyle "pioneers" did nothing of the sort; they reconstructed new family forms not because they desired to blaze new social trails but because the constraints of work and the value placed on success altered the practice of their daily lives. (p. 197)

The intense and focused commitment of time required to meet the expectations for tenure at most universities is an example of how the requirements of work shape the daily lives and lifestyles of academics during early career.

While it is the most common form of cross-sex collaboration (Kaufman, 1978), the risks of collaborating with a spouse have particularly negative repercussions for women. Women generally receive less recognition when they publish with men (Loeb, 2001). This is even more so the case for women collaborating with a spouse (Rossiter, 1993). Part of the explanation for this lies in a phenomenon, labeled by R. K. Merton as the Matthew Effect, where well-known scholars or those considered to have more expertise receive considerably more credit than they often deserve for work done with others and "sometimes even for work for which they were not responsible at all" (Loeb, p. 171). This is one reason why early-career faculty members, male and female alike, are encouraged to cut formal ties with a mentor and to establish an independent identity before collaborating. This explains why women most often chose to collaborate with other women where issues of credit and recognition are less likely to be clouded by differences in status.

Transitioning to Faculty Life

Academics face a number of decisions as they transition to a faculty role that has long-term significance not only for their career trajectory but also for their personal relationships. These include the decision to enter a committed relationship, the type of job to accept, and the strategies to employ to meet the demands for career advancement. These decisions are even thornier for academic couples, particularly for those with overlapping areas of expertise, as they face an even more restricted labor market than their peers who are unmarried or married to someone in a different field.

Academic couples described a number of ways that their career aspirations shaped the decision to commit to a long-term personal relationship.

The Attraction

The explanations coworking couples offered for the decision to enter a committed relationship and to collaborate were often intertwined. Probably because most of these couples met during graduate school when their vocational identities had emerged, these relationships were shaped by a career focus, shared interests, and expectations about the lifestyle demanded by an academic career. Collaboration offered these couples a way to juggle a personal relationship and a demanding career.

Early vocational identity is evident in how Anna[2] describes the decision to marry in 1974. Characterizing herself and her spouse, Roger, as being "terminally tongue tied" about talking about their personal relationship, Anna, an endowed professor of psychology, made it clear that their career ambitions came first in their relationship.

> There was no question about one of us giving up on our careers. We were too committed to our work to consider that. The relationship could have gone either way.

When Anna said that the relationship "could have gone either way" she meant that the decision to continue their relationship and marry only came after they were both able to secure suitable faculty positions.

The strong role of career interests in the decision to marry is also evident in the account of Opal and Cliff, who first met in the early 1970s when she was a doctoral student and he was her professor. Characterizing herself as a person who developed a compulsive and competitive orientation through her involvement with debate in high school, Opal, a professor of communication studies, said,

> I wonder if in part you have some people who were naturally, compulsively motivated to produce in the first place and so, perhaps, my finding a mate who also had the same tendencies, it made it easier for them to keep doing that because they had a mate who wasn't constantly after them to stop.

Opal is suggesting that part of what attracted her to her husband was that he would not get in the way of her strong work orientation.

Given the priority of work in the lives of these coworking couples, it is not surprising that an opportunity to talk about shared interests and to pursue ideas was central, not only to the attraction that launched these relationships but also to sustaining them. Self-labeled as a human geographer, Martha talked about her initial attraction to her partner, Greg, in terms of a shared interest in the "life of the mind." Describing this, she said,

> Both of us are driven by ideas. Both of us are very content, and have been all of our lives, with the excitement of the life of the mind. It makes us very compatible because it is something that we can really understand about each other. Many other people do not understand it very much. . . . It's a philosophy about what life is about.

Martha, a geography professor, spent the first part of her career with another male partner who shared her intellectual interests. In finding a mate to collaborate with, Martha is living a fantasy that merges a private and public life. Even as a teenager, she imagined herself sitting down at the breakfast table with a partner and having an animated conversation about work.

For some couples, the experience of collaborating allows them access to the qualities that brought them to admire and respect their partner's skills and intellect in the first place. Thirty years after their relationship began, Aleesha, now a prominent feminist sociologist, said that she and her partner, Virgil, have always had the habit of reading and commenting on each other's work. She said she enjoys writing with her partner because

> It makes me like him because when we sit down to work on something together, I see the side of him that I like and admire a lot and that I liked and admired when I first met him. It taps into this part. I am impressed by the things that he knows that I don't know.

Deeply shared intellectual interests are at the root of these relationships. Whether acknowledged informally through feedback about manuscripts or formally through coauthorship on publications, collaboration offered these couples a way to advance their career goals while sustaining a personal life. They accomplished their career goals not in the traditional way, by keeping a distinction between their personal and private lives, but in the nontraditional way of merging their private and public lives through scholarly collaboration. These relationships did not drive research productivity as much as it allowed it to unfold.

The Compact to Keep It Equal

The couples in my sample looked back on the early days of their relationship and point to an agreement that was implicitly or explicitly negotiated about the priority of their careers. One aspect of the agreement was that work was central to their identities and lives. A second aspect was an agreement to "keep it equal," generally by taking turns in accepting opportunities, with the intent of advancing both careers. The centrality of work, not the relationship, is what is important about this agreement. The decision to coauthor was often a natural outgrowth of shared interests and the commitment to support each other's careers and to keep it equal.

For some couples, a vow to keep it equal was part of the initial commitment they made to each other. Ideology was at the root of some of these commitments; pragmatic reasons drove others. Laura, an anthropologist, who coauthored a book with her husband that appeared in print just about the time she was being reviewed for tenure, described the ideological basis of their relationship in the early 1980s. She said, "A deep philosophical commitment to egalitarianism marked the beginning of our relationship." Another couple's commitment to keep it equal was less ideological and more pragmatic. Roxanne, one of a pair of psychologists, acknowledged that she and her husband, Stuart, set out to maintain comparable records so that neither one of them would be seen as the "trailing partner."

> There was an element of competition. Also in that we knew that if we wanted to move on in our careers, we were going to have to stay close to each other in terms of our level of visibility and productivity. We didn't want to have the feeling of one person tagging along after the other.

For some, the goal of awarding equal priority to both careers meant the couple adopted the strategy that they would take turns taking advantage of opportunities that came their way. For a pair of geologists, Sally and Ed, who married in the late 1960s, Sally described the compact they reached:

> That had been our agreement from the very beginning. Before we were married, before we even got engaged, we sat down and talked. How are we going to do this if we get married? Should we just "live in sin" or just split and go our own ways or what? We decided we wanted to stay together more than anything and if we would stay together if would mean somebody would have to sacrifice; that we would take turns sacrificing. The relationship started as co-equal from the beginning.

Sally, now a full professor, and Ed, who holds a temporary appointment, have never had the luxury of holding comparable positions. In the context of a very tight job market, they approached their relationship with the assumption that in order to keep their careers balanced they would have to take turns sacrificing.

The compact these coworking couples made and the strategies they deployed to promote their own and each other's careers met with varying degrees of success during their early career. Their early commitment to mutuality often came into conflict with the ethic of competitive individualism that is deeply embedded in the reward and recognition systems of research universities.

The Compact Meets the Ethic of Competitive Individualism

Coworking couples reported that they received a variety of warnings from colleagues and department heads about the risks associated with collaborating with someone they shared an intimate relationship with. The message underlying these exchanges was often about "who did what," with the colleague assuming that these couples had a clear division of labor and the ability to apportion differing levels of credit. Some women encountered the implicit or explicit charge that the male member of the pair must be doing the work. One of the most consistent themes to emerge across the collaborative accounts was the experience of being admonished about the importance of an independent research identity. Some couples appeared to be aware of the power of this injunction from the earliest days of their faculty careers. For example, Roger, a member of a couple hired in the same psychology department at the same time, said, "We were sensitive of that from the beginning and knew we needed to establish beyond a shadow of a doubt that each of us had an independent line of research that we were identified with." Participants seemed to feel this even more acutely when there was a career gap, even when the gap was as little as two years. Roxanne, a psychologist working in the same department, said, "For me, personally, it was critical that I establish an area independent of him because he was a couple of years further along."

Coworking couples described a variety of ways that their intellectual autonomy was challenged. Couples in the same department seemed particularly susceptible to questions about "who did what." "There is some perception on some people's part that you don't publish with your spouse because then you can't tell who really did the work," Alex, a member of a pair of special educators observed. Other couples were sensitive to the implication that one was "carrying the other" because there was really only enough work for one. Melanie, Alex's partner, described what she considered to be mixed messages about collaborating.

> I felt like at some times we were being given mixed messages because we were told that it was better to collaborate than to write individually, and

at other times we were told you need to write individually also. At this point, within our department and coming from the college level, we were actually asked to, by work, identify what our role had been in the effort. . . . I think they thought one of us was carrying the other.

Several women encountered the implicit or explicit charge that the male member of the pair was the one really doing the work. Samantha, a sociologist, stressed the pressure she and her husband felt to have distinct career trajectories after entering comparable faculty positions in the early 1970s. "Because we felt at that point in history women were very disadvantaged and it would be very easy to be seen as in your husband's shadow." Those who escaped questions about their intellectual autonomy were those whose spouse was not an academic or was in an area so far removed that even the most uninformed outsider would not have trouble distinguishing their individual contributions.

Even faculty whose record of awards during their early career clearly marked them as superstars in the making faced challenges about their intellectual autonomy. Although she downplayed it by labeling it as only a "small chunk of the total picture," Opal has the astonishing record of publishing 4 of 10 books, 6 of 26 chapters, and 33 of 112 journal articles with her spouse, Cliff. When I asked her if she had encountered situations where people made assumptions about their coauthored work, she said,

> Absolutely. In fact, after I had [won] about the third or fourth top paper award, there was one person who said, this can't be . . . what's the probability of that happening . . . it must be because of my connections with my spouse. Of course, these are papers that are read blind, but here's this person insinuating that somehow my achievements weren't due to my own efforts.

Opal's astonishing overall publication record probably deflected questions about the significant amount of work coauthored with a spouse that might have arisen in a less extraordinary case.

Accommodations to the Expectations for Tenure

Prior to earning tenure, couples used a number of different strategies to respond to the questions about their intellectual autonomy. This included concealing their relationship, downplaying the amount they collaborated, maintaining unusually symmetrical records, or developing such a strong publication record that the collaboration was no longer an issue. After earning tenure and developing a strong publication record, several couples had the intellectual capital to relocate to a more prestigious institution. Others avoided the issue entirely by postponing any formal recognition of collaboration until after earning the security of tenure.

Concealing the Relationship

Sally and Ed, geologists, and Anna and Roger, psychologists, are couples who have sustained common research interests for decades. They are also similar in that both couples not only completed degrees from the same department, but they did it under the supervision of the same advisor. Entering tight job markets at different times, both concealed their relationship during the job interview process. Sally, now a professor at a midwestern university, said, "In 1983, you didn't have a spouse. You could live in sin, but you couldn't have a spouse." Anna and Roger, who secured comparable positions at another research university in the Midwest in the mid-1970s, also concealed their relationship during the interview process. Explaining that decision, Roger said, "It was a deliberate decision on my part. It is not that we lied about it; it is just that we chose to keep quiet about it. The reason I decided that was because the year before, a woman in the department had tried to get her spouse hired and it complicated things. It seemed to me certainly it was not going to do any good and it had the potential to do some harm."

Downplay the Amount of Collaboration

Anna's and Roger's attempts to be strategic during the interview process extended to their early career. While always engaged in giving each other feedback about manuscripts, they sidestepped issues that might cloud recognition by not listing themselves as coauthors on any publications prior to earning tenure. Roger's words reflect how attuned they were to the injunction against collaboration:

> We did some collaboration fairly early on, but it is also true that we worked hard at establishing our own separate careers. . . . The hazards in the department that we were in and a lot of departments like that is that any long-term collaborative relationship, the question arises, well whose is this

really? There's this belief there is only enough there for one. It is particularly a hazard if you have a long-term collaboration with your advisor and a long-term collaboration with a spouse just draws those inferences. So, we were sensitive of that from the beginning and knew that we needed to establish beyond a shadow of a doubt that each of us had an independent line of research that we were identified with. We did collaborate within the first few years of being faculty members but it was only on the third lines of research that weren't within either of our individual areas.

Despite Roger's references to collaborating within the first few years of being faculty members, no publications with both of their names appears on either of their curricula vitae prior to the year they earned tenure. Like their decision to conceal their relationship during their job interviews, it seems likely that they sought to avoid complications by not appearing as coauthors on any publications prior to earning tenure.

Another couples' publication records also raise the suspicion that they underreported their collaboration. The meteoric rise in Opal's total publication count and coauthored publication count in the four short years between tenure (1980, 3 of 15 coauthored with her spouse) and achieving full professor (1984, 22 of 61 coauthored with her spouse) seems only possible through the contributions of a team of collaborators, including graduate students. It seems likely that Opal underreported the amount of work she collaborated on.

Redirecting a Research Agenda

Members of other coworking couples who collaborated prior to earning tenure later chose to redirect their research agenda to combat some of the questions they faced about intellectual autonomy. This was the case for sociologist Aleesha. Despite the fact that it quickly became apparent that her productivity would far outpace her husband's, Aleesha chose to move away from the topic of her dissertation, which was an area of interest she shared with her husband, Virgil. Of her decision to redirect her research agenda, Aleesha said,

I think that one of the reasons I moved away from [the topic of her dissertation], in fact which is what I did my early work in, was because I wanted to be in a different domain. I didn't want to be [hesitation] . . . not just for practical reasons, such as that people might not give me credit for my work, but just because the differentiation was . . . I didn't want to be the clone or little sister of this person who was already well established. I am a competitive person, much more than he is. I think that it was partly that as well.

Despite the investment in time it took to develop expertise in another topic, Aleesha responded to pressure to distinguish herself from her husband not only to get credit for her work but also, in order to advance in her career, by redirecting her research agenda. The lag time it took her to retool was costly not only to her but to her institution.

"Dazzle" Them with the Numbers

Some couples were able to counter the criticism their collaboration generated by developing such strong publication records that the collaboration became a moot issue. This was the case, for example, for special educator Alex who came up to tenure with a total of 31 publications, 14 coauthored with his wife, Melanie. Resistant to the admonition he received from his department head to reduce how much he collaborated, Alex admitted, "I did it my way and because I did enough of it, you know, I dazzled them [with] my numbers a little bit, so to speak. So I got by with it." Similarly, psychologist Roxanne said that her publications with her husband, Stuart, were of such strength and quality that

> By the time we got tenure there, we both had pretty substantial vitas and so you can begin to say well, but you have all of these overlapping publications. But at least in our case, the schools were smart enough to realize that as long as we continued to be productive, whether it was jointly or singly, it didn't matter.

In this case, the institutional context was such that their collaboration was not devalued.

A strong publication record seemed to have provided some women with the leverage to relocate to other universities that they perceived to be more couple friendly. Anna, the cognitive psychologist, accepted an invitation to apply for a faculty position, an endowed chair, at a university in the Midwest on the condition that a position was available for her partner, Roger. Anna and Roger negotiated appointments in different departments as a strategy to avoid some of the departmental politics their relationship had engendered at their previous institution. Similarly, Roxanne and Stuart, another pair of psychologists, escaped departmental politics after earning tenure by relocating to a more prestigious institution. Like Anna, the move was made at Roxanne's initiation, in response to a vacancy for a senior woman, but she said,

> It has turned out that the career moves we have made have really been at my instigation, which is kind of ironic because I think that if you just put down objective indicators, he has the better record of the two of us in terms of publications.

Roxanne's statement is a bit perplexing given that she and her husband, Stuart, have been able to hold true to their original pledge to keep it equal by maintaining publication records over the first ten years of their careers that are too symmetrical to be coincidental.

Summary

Fortunately for the well-being of these work-driven relationships, the influence of the reward and recognition system on the personal relationship diminished after the intense period during early careers that marks the bid for tenure. By that point, the injunction against collaboration diminished and, at the same time, most couples had clearly differentiated their research agendas. Anna noted the shift in priorities in the reward structure when she said, "We're both full professors now. . . . All of the issues that were important at the beginning of us keeping separate identities are no longer important. We both have very separate identities as professionals and, for the most part, aside from the most general kinds of conferences, we don't even go to the same meetings."

Demonstrating intellectual autonomy is an extra burden faced by dual-career academic couples, particularly during the years prior to earning tenure. Despite vivid accounts of encounters with colleagues questioning their intellectual autonomy, all of the faculty members in tenure-track positions were tenured and most were promoted. As judged by the awards and honors listed on their vitae, many have achieved considerable prominence in their field. Part of this reflects their early acumen in gauging the requirements of the academic reward structure.

That it was invariably the woman who repeatedly referred to the importance of establishing an identity distinct from her spouse during the early part of their careers suggests that issues of intellectual autonomy continue to present greater challenges to women who collaborate with a spouse than for men in the same situation, just as has been documented in the past (e.g., Kaufman, 1978; Russ, 1983). While both members of such couples may mutually benefit in the long run from the human capital of their partner, as suggested by Xie and Shauman (1998), this is not necessarily a benefit that manifests itself in the same way for all dual-career couples.

Conclusion

Some authors have suggested that spousal hiring policies keep academic couples together (Wolf-Wendel, Twombly, & Rice, 2000). The accounts presented in this chapter suggest that while hiring policies may serve initially to increase the likelihood that couples will be able to sustain a relationship and a family, the individualistic values implicit in the academic reward structure at most colleges and universities are equally likely to pull them apart. Issues of recognition and reward had a significant impact on the experiences of the sample of dual-career academics in this study, often appearing to come into conflict with the commitment to promote each other's career ambitions and to keep it equal, which marked their early marriage compact. A partner in the same field, particularly when faculty appointments are in the same department, probably exacerbates the requirement to establish an independent scholarly identity that presents such a major career hurdle for early-career faculty.

The strength of the individualistic values of the reward structure is evident in the range of evasive strategies couples deployed in response to the injunction to establish an independent, scholarly identity. These include to conceal or to downplay the personal relationship, understate collaboration rates, maintain impeccably symmetrical publication records, "dazzle" with numbers, and to realign a research agenda to avoid suspicion about their intellectual autonomy. That acrimonious departmental politics led some couples to relocate in search of a more couple-friendly environment is a further indication of the power of the reward structure and peer censure in shaping life trajectories.

The bias that couples are likely to collude to elevate their publication counts by *overstating* the contribution of a partner, is countered by findings that suggest that it is probably more likely that they *understate* the amount they collaborate in order to sidestep questions about their intellectual independence. This leads me to the ironic speculation that the failure to acknowledge the intellectual contributions of a spouse, graduate student, or colleague is probably far less likely to go unchallenged when judgments are made about their productivity than the decision to acknowledge the significance of the contributions of contributors through coauthorship.

The commitment required to earn tenure at a competitive research university has been compared to making partner in a law firm (Barnett & Hyde, 2001). The nature of faculty work and the intellectual creativity and persistence required to advance knowledge require a commitment of time and psychological resources that intrude on the time even the most work-oriented might set aside for personal and family pursuits. These demands are at the base of my argument that academic leaders should reimagine the faculty reward system as a work/family policy that shapes faculty lives as much as it does careers. Like spousal hiring policies, promotion and tenure policies should be reviewed to maximize an individual's potential for productivity. Removing barriers to collaboration, including artificial restraints to collaboration among those who share a personal or long-term relationship at early career, is one step in the right direction.

External funding agencies may be helping to promote what is nothing short of a culture shift in higher education. As the corporate world has shifted to a culture that values and rewards teamwork, so higher education can benefit by redesigning the reward structure to give top awards to the accomplishments of teams that advance the careers of all its members. Attention to work/family policies, including how promotion and tenure policies affect the productivity of dual-career academic couples, is one way institutions can maximize the potential for productivity of its faculty and communicate a commitment to the success of individual faculty members.

References

Astin, H. S., & Milem, J. F. (1997). The status of academic couples in U.S. institutions. In M. A. Ferber and J. W. Loeb (Eds.), *Academic couples: Problems and promises* (pp. 128–155). Urbana: University of Illinois Press.

Barnett, R. C., & Hyde, J. S. (2001). Women, men, work, and family: An expansionist theory. *American Psychologist, 56*(10), 781–796.

Bird, G. W., & Bird, G. A. (1987). In pursuit of academic careers: Observations of a dual-career couple. *Family Relations, 36,* 97–100.

Creamer, E. G., & Associates. (2001). *Working equal: Academic couples as collaborators.* New York: RoutledgeFalmer.

Fox, M. F. (2004). Georgia Tech ADVANCE Survey of Faculty Perceptions, Needs, and Experiences. Retrieved from http://www.advance.gatech.edu/measure.html

Fox, M. F., & Faver, C. A. (1984). Independence and cooperation in research: The motivations and costs of collaboration. *Journal of Higher Education, 55*(3), 347–359.

Goodman, N., Royce, E., Selvin, H. C., & Weinstein, E. A. (1984). The academic couples in sociology: Managing greedy institutions. In W. W. Powell & R. Robbins (Eds.), *Conflict and consensus: A festschrift in honor of Lewis A. Coser.* New York: Free Press.

Hochschild, A. R. (1997). *The time bind: When work becomes home and home becomes work.* New York: Henry Holt.

John-Steiner, V. (1997). *Notebooks of the mind: Explorations of thinking.* New York: Oxford University Press.

John-Steiner, V. (2000). *Creative collaboration.* New York: Oxford University Press.

Kaufman, D. R. (1978). Associational ties in academe: Some male and female differences. *Sex Roles, 4*(1), 9–21.

Loeb, J. W. (2001). The role of recognition and reward in research productivity: Implications for partner collaboration. In E. G. Creamer & Associates, *Working equal: Academic couples as collaborators* (pp. 167–185). New York: RoutledgeFalmer.

Norrell, J. E., & Norrell, T. H. (1996). Faculty and family policies in higher education. *Journal of Family Issues, 17,* 204–226.

Perry, R., & Brownley, M. W. (Eds.). (1984). *Mothering the mind: Twelve studies of writers and their silent partners.* New York: Holmes and Meier.

Risman, B. J. (1998). *Gender vertigo: American families in transition.* New Haven, CT: Yale University Press.

Rose, P. (1994). *Parallel lives: Five Victorian marriages.* New York: Vintage Press.

Rossiter, M. W. (1993). The Matilda effect in science. *Social Studies of Science, 23*(2), 325–341.

Russ, J. (1983). *How to suppress women's writing.* Austin: University of Texas Press.

Scanzoni, L., & Scanzoni, J. (1976). *Men, women, and change: A sociology of marriage and family.* New York: McGraw-Hill.

Schwartz, P. (1994). *Love between equals: How peer marriages really work.* New York: Free Press.

Smart, M. S., & Smart, R. C. (1990). Paired prospects: Dual career couples on campus. *Academe 76*(1), pp. 33–37.

Trower, C. A., Austin, A. E., & Sorcinelli, M. D. (May 2001). Paradise lost: How the academy converts enthusiasm recruits into early-career doubters. *AAHE Bulletin, 53*(9), 3–6.

Wolf-Wendel, L., Twombly, S., & Rice, S. (2000). Dual career couples: Keeping them together. *Journal of Higher Education, 71,* 291–321.

Xie, Y., & Shauman, K. A. (1998). Sex differences in research productivity: New evidence about an old puzzle. *American Sociological Review, 63,* 847–870.

Notes

1. Even though there are no same-sex pairs in the sample I describe in this chapter, I use the words "couple" and "partners" interchangeably as a way to avoid marginalizing the experiences of same-sex couples.

2. Full-length case studies of three of the couples mentioned in this paper (Martha and Greg, Anna and Roger, and Laura and Allen, appear in my book, *Working Equal: Academic Couples as Collaborators.*

5

AGENTS OF LEARNING

Strategies for Assuming Agency, for Learning, in Tenured Faculty Careers

Anna Neumann, Aimee LaPointe Terosky, and Julie Schell

W hat happens to professors' job and career demands after tenure? Given the intensity of the probationary years and the tenure review (Tierney & Bensimon, 1996) we might expect high-tension career demands to "lighten up" after tenure. In the common view, tenured professors are free to construct their work as they wish, emphasizing or de-emphasizing their teaching, research, outreach, and service at will. However, our analysis of interviews with 40 recently tenured professors, representing diverse disciplines and fields and working at four major research universities in the United States, reveals that career demands do not lessen with tenure. Quite the contrary, they increase, notably in service, administration, and outreach (Neumann & Terosky, 2003). The increase is exacerbated by the newness of these tasks to many professors who, prior to tenure, were shielded from organizational work. To fulfill these new posttenure responsibilities, professors must learn what they entail, how to carry them out, and not least, how to orchestrate them with their other academic responsibilities, including their scholarly learning (Neumann & Terosky, 2003). Tenured professors may also need to learn how to teach a broader array of courses and students than they did as junior faculty. Others may need to learn new skills as they assume collaborative, administrative, and leadership responsibilities in re-

The research reported in this paper was made possible by a grant from the Spencer Foundation and a faculty research fellowship from Teachers College, Columbia University. The data presented, the statements made, and the views expressed are solely the responsibility of the authors.

search, university or professional association governance, editorial work, and other domains in which they have little or no prior experience. This learning for increased professional responsibility is a major challenge of the early post-tenure career. Typically, it happens "on the job," requiring close coordination of *doing* and *learning to do*.

The management of this posttenure learning is complex because it is not confined to any one domain of professors' work. Rather, the need to learn pervades professors' work across the board: their teaching, research, service, and outreach. Thus after tenure any aspect (or all aspects) of professors' work may assume a new form. As such, newly tenured professors may face abundant "new work" that, in addition to doing, they must also learn to do. The learning will, of course, differ by person, field of study, local culture, and subject of learning. Despite such differences, virtually all professors participating in our study struggled with this challenge: how to coordinate or balance the learning that drew them to lives of scholarly study and teaching in the first place, with new demands to learn new things, both related and unrelated to their scholarly interests.

Given the changed landscape of work in the early posttenure career, we wondered: How do recently tenured professors, who encounter a surfeit of new professional demands manage? How do they carry out new tasks while learning about them, and while continuing also in the learning that their scholarship requires? Our analysis of 40 recently tenured university professors' descriptions of their learning and their work suggests the following: Recently tenured professors who *respond strategically* to increased demands, in the form of work and learning, can invent useful ways to manage expanding work expectations, increasing calls to learn new work, and often, growing desires to continue in their scholarly learning. *Strategic response* may be construed as personal and self-directed meaning-making amid an otherwise disordered, even chaotic informational setting (Schutz, 1970; Weick, 1979)— one's efforts to interpret and arrange one's reality (the setting of work and/or life) to render it sensible to oneself, for example, by chunking it up and ordering it in ways that "make sense," and pursuing one's goals within this reformed reality. We use the sociological concept of *agency* to underline the personal, self-directed meaning-making effort, though realizing that it occurs, virtually always, with and among others, that is, in social context (Berger & Luckmann, 1966). In exerting agency, individuals garner power, will, and desire to create work contexts conducive to the development of their thought over time (see Elder, 1997, 964–965). In our view, then, *agency*, lies at the heart of *strategic response.*

In this chapter, we present three cases of professors' strategic responses to posttenure demands for increased learning and work—the scholarly and perhaps not-so-scholarly, and their intermingling, with close attention to professors' efforts to interweave these purposefully in mutually supportive ways. We thereby emphasize the agential qualities of professors' responses to new work through the early posttenure career, and consider implications for professors' learning.

Agency as a Framework for Understanding Tenured Academic Careers

The concept of agency has guided the study of human lives since the early 1900s (Elder, 1994). Sociological and psychological theories of agency provide insight into how individuals develop throughout their lives, and how in some cases, individuals may position themselves to pilot their own development (Lerner & Busch-Rossnagel, 1981), at least partially. Despite the unique and varied circumstances they are born into and live in, individuals can and do influence their own life trajectories in intentional ways (Clausen, 1991; Elder, 1994; Lerner & Busch-Rossnagel, 1981; Marshall, 2000). According to Baltes and Baltes (1990), acts of self-creation do not cease in childhood or early adulthood; they continue through the course of life.

What, then, is *agency* as applied to the human life course, and what does it reveal about professors' lives? We define *agency* as "the human capacity . . . to act intentionally, planfully and reflexively and in a temporal or a biographical mode," and as reflecting the presumption that "all human beings have free will" (Marshall, 2000, p. 11). We emphasize forms of agency that influence the content of human development, how individuals can, in a sense, become agents of their own learning and development, thereby coming into identities consciously or willingly chosen or crafted. Yet we acknowledge, too, that "some individuals . . . are more effective than others in making positive events happen in the course of their development" (Clausen, 1991, p. 810). Effectiveness in activating agency in desirable ways may relate to the resources available to individuals (Marshall, 2000). For example, wealthy people are likely to have greater access to culturally valued resources and alternative courses of action than the impoverished (Elder, 1999). Similarly, members of privileged cultural strata may have more or better access to culturally defined intellectual resources associated with cultural dominance than individuals whose cultural currencies do not equate with the prevailing "cultural capital" (Bourdieu, 1986). We also acknowledge that individual actions, and hence lives, are significantly regulated by external influences and institutions (e.g., Buchmann, 1989; Mayer & Schoepflin, 1989; Neugarten, Moore, & Lowe, 1965; O'Rand, 1996, 2000; Sorensen, 1986), and indeed, that agency is entwined with social structure, as acting freely takes place in the context of a structure that presents various opportunities and constraints (Elder, 1994).

We may, therefore, view agency as a product of the larger social world even as by definition agency strives to change that world, to reform it in line with the "meanings" and "sense" of an "agent"—a person (professor) who fashions a particular context (one's academic and intellectual workspace) as a location for that person's meaning-making efforts (products of professorial work). Given patterns of social stratification, individuals vary in their access to context-embedded resources and privileges, and in their abilities to draw on such resources for meaning-making. Their efforts to act as agents of their own minds—to create contexts conducive to their meaning-making, and thereby their learning—may, in some cases, be stumped or diverted. We deem it important that all tenured professors develop abilities to think and act, strategically, with agency. As we suggest later, we deem it important also that they have access to resources for doing so.

In light of this view, we must ask how individuals activate a sense of agency to influence their lives effectively in settings that are new to them or that change, literally, underfoot, for example, as these individuals assume new status, responsibility, and power. Such is the case of recently tenured professors whose work, and work expectations, change in the early posttenure career (see Neumann & Terosky, 2003). As one's work changes, so does the nature of one's work context, and so does one's role and agency within it (Neumann, 1999c). We therefore ask: What are some ways in which professors, encountering the "newness" of the posttenure career, can employ agency to influence the content and/or structure of their work (for example, in achieving a desirable relationship between their scholarly learning and other professional learning they must engage in), given the opportunities and constraints of the tenured academic profession and of the particular institutional and disciplinary environments these professors work in day by day?

We suggest that *agency* is an important concept for addressing this question because of its definitional proximity to *learning*. *To learn* is to formulate fresh insight—to make sense of something unknown or unclear—from within one's self. Learning requires thinking, acting, and speaking from honest acknowledgment of what a learner does and does not know about a particular subject. Learning, if it is to be more than unthinking adaptation to the common view (see Dannefer & Perlmutter, 1990), requires attentiveness to the "truth" of one's perceptions and sense-making. Both agency and learning require a person—as agent and learner—to attend to the voice of that person's internal meaning-making. Thus agency can be viewed as supportive and constitutive of a constructivist vision of learning.[1] Assuming that learning, and teaching others to learn, is central to professors' work (Kerr, 1995), we deem agency, as part of learning, as central as well.

In the remainder of the chapter, we describe the research that yielded this view of agency in recently tenured professors' careers. We then present three cases of newly tenured professors assuming agency in their work. We close with an agenda for future research on learning, strategy, and agency in professors' careers and lives.

Design and Method

This chapter derives from a 3-year longitudinal study of professors' learning and development in the early posttenure career.[2] Forty professors (20 women, 20 men), representing the sciences (11), social sciences (9), arts and humanities (9), and professional/applied fields (11), and working at four major research (Carnegie Classified Doctoral/Research University–Extensive) universities throughout the United States, participated in two-hour, on-site interviews carried out in project years 1 and 3. Professors had been tenured and promoted to the rank of associate professor within three years of the first interview. Thus by the second interview, they were between three and five years posttenure. A small proportion had been promoted to full professor and a sizable number was planning to come up for promotion within a year or two.

Core study data include full transcripts of year-1 and year-3 interviews focusing on professors' representations of their work, lives, and careers. Subsidiary data—culled from professors' scholarly products (CVs, publications, tenure narratives), observational notes, campus documents, interviews with administrators and senior faculty leaders, and public sources—provide views of professors' careers, institutional cultures and priorities, and work conditions. During data analysis, we engaged in several rounds of close reading of interview transcripts, followed by comparative reviews aimed at conceptualization of strategies for assuming agency in academic contexts. Our analytic approach borrows heavily from grounded theory (Glaser & Strauss, 1967), a research tradition that purports to induce theory from a "ground" of untheorized data, though as conditioned by extant perspectives on the subject of study (see Schatzman & Strauss, 1973 for discussions of theoretical mediation in qualitative research). The perspectives that conditioned our analysis derive from sociological and social psychological studies of the life course.

Strategies for Assuming Agency in the Early Posttenure Career: Cases in Point

We explore how newly tenured professors who face abundant learning tasks strategize their learning with the following question in mind: how to organize one's work life to maximize support for scholarly learning that holds meaning for the professor as learner? We rely on theories of agency to frame the following three strategies:

- Putting it together: integrating as many parts of one's work life as possible around a substantive focus that matters—professionally, intellectually, and personally
- Containment (or learning to learn in small spaces): narrowing one's scholarly work so it can be managed, yet ensuring that in its restricted form it retains substance to be learned
- Invoking design: creating orderly environments that promote resourcefulness and self-sufficiency, thereby limiting distractions and conserving reserves of personal energy and time for scholarly learning

We elaborate on these strategies through the narratives of three recently tenured professors.

Strategy 1: Integrating as Many Parts of One's Work Life as Possible Around a Substantive Focus That Matters—Professionally, Intellectually, and Personally

Many of the professors in our study talk and think about their work in traditional terms, separating research, teaching, and service as distinct and mutually exclusive. They may, then, couple their own learning as scholars to research while linking students' learning to teaching. In doing so, they decouple their own and their students' learning; they separate the knowledge construction of research from the knowledge construction of teaching. However, some participating professors conceptualize their jobs differently. Some openly break with the traditional practice of sharply dividing research, teaching, and service from one other. Others go even further, declaring that they themselves can learn substantively about their subjects of study, not only in their research, but also in their teaching, service, and/or outreach. These professors may see themselves as learning with, among, and from those they teach and serve. In these professors' views, teaching and learning (subject-matter anchored) overlap, as do the roles of teacher and learner. Distinctions among research, teaching, and service blur at points where opportunities to engage in subject-matter learning (others' and their own) predominate. These professors make room, in effect, for a stream of common content (the subjects, issues, and questions that they care about and seek to learn) to traverse and bind their diverse work activities. Thus they may learn about a topic in one way in their research, in another way while teaching, and in yet a third way while carrying out outreach and service. All these activities may serve as "places of learning" for the professor.

Recalling our interviews with professors who think in this way about their work, we summon up the image of a stream of substantive learning. The shape, content, and current of the stream is unique for each professor. It "carries" different knowledge, questions, and ways of knowing and inquiring. It courses through, and binds, different parts of the academic terrain. For some professors, the stream binds only selected aspects of research and teaching, outreach and research, and so on, but for others, it connects more. Our starkest and most comprehensive example is this: The stream feeds a professor's research, permeates that individual's teaching, and directs that person's choice of service, outreach, and administrative projects, both inside and outside the university. Though the 40 professors in our study vary in the comprehensiveness of such "binding," some do integrate their work thoroughly, making it hard to tell where their research, teaching, outreach, and service leave off and begin. The case of Elizabeth Ferrara is a prime example of a professor who merges research, teaching (including mentoring), and outreach with aims of advancing her own and others' learning.

Elizabeth exemplifies well the professor who assumes agency, through integration, across a broad swath of her academic work. Elizabeth studies gerontology with emphasis on social policy directed at the welfare of the elderly. Over the years, she has successfully merged a well-funded research program, full teaching portfolio, and diverse institutional service and outreach projects she has been deeply committed to. How has she done this? Rather than relying on logistics, organizational schemes, timelines, and other bureaucratic tools to line up her diverse responsibilities, Elizabeth uses content—common questions and issues that she can pursue diversely, but relatedly, across the multiple settings of her work: in research groups, in teaching situations including classrooms, in external community service projects, in professional association work, and so on. For example, Elizabeth focuses her research on some large-scale social concerns about the quality of life for the aged in our society. Yet she realizes that these large-scale social issues manifest themselves locally. Her outreach projects typically involve individuals and communities likely to benefit from her unique substantive knowledge of those social issues, and from whom she, too, may benefit from close-up observation. For example, as part of her outreach endeavor, she may observe local policy implementation, or she may design a field experiment that tests two or more competing modes of service provision, a project useful to the site and helpful for theory testing and development within her own research agenda.

Elizabeth folds her scholarly learning, similarly, into her teaching, thereby creating a subject-matter-driven pedagogy that is tied to the substantive concerns of her research and outreach. As she describes her teaching, Elizabeth notes that her outreach to community programs, along with her research on these programs, has reshaped her teaching. She says:

> [In my field] . . . you need to be leaders, you need to be entrepreneurial, you need to be risk-takers, and if you have them sitting in class, and you are showing a colon, that's the wrong message. And at the same time, saying it is important to network and it is important to take initiative, so I've tried to change the rules in my classroom, to encourage students to participate in their own learning, to have learning agendas . . . breaking them into groups, doing role plays, and doing exercises. And part of that has come from my work with [community groups/health service people].

As this example suggests, Elizabeth's teaching has developed in response to her learning through her research and outreach. Further, Elizabeth often brings into class her own research problems and cases to help convey conceptual understanding. By looking closely at the details of real cases, students may of their own accord derive underlying principles that otherwise she as the professor would have to present more abstractly through lecture (though sometimes she does). As is evident from this discussion, Elizabeth's teaching draws on her research and outreach, and thus the three—teaching, research, outreach—are related in her career.

But there is more to be said about what comes of the teaching-outreach-research linkages that Elizabeth establishes: Not only does she gain for her teaching from her research and outreach, but the converse occurs as well, for example, as she learns substantively from students, both graduates and undergraduates, for her research and outreach. In one of her interviews, Elizabeth described how her research was suddenly jeopardized when the providers of the service she was investigating changed. Given new provider initiatives, her established study design seemed on the verge of crumbling; she stood to lose a number of important study sites. Elizabeth pondered: How might the project be salvaged? One of Elizabeth's students who was familiar with the system at issue counseled her through the difficulty. Elizabeth summarizes this student's contribution to her project as critical: "what he had done really helped us rescue our study." Some time later, the student signed up for advanced research methods courses, and through his learning there, contributed significant strengths to Elizabeth's research team, much as other of Elizabeth's students typically do. She notes, "my expectations are that they [students] become experts in these areas [within her project] and really contribute to me and to the research teams."

While it may not be unusual for professors to learn from students working on their research projects, it is rare to hear of professors learning authentically in classrooms—that is, in the context of their teaching. Yet Elizabeth unabashedly uses her classes, graduate and undergraduate, in this way. For example, she refers to a particular teaching experience of hers as "a great course for me to learn [the subject] as part of my [professional] retooling." "The great thing is that there are a lot of books that have been published in the last couple of years, so reading those, and then assigning them was really helpful to me. And organizing the material was very helpful," she explains. Through our discussion, Elizabeth referred also to classroom teaching experiences and reading assignments that have supported her application for and conduct of a state-funded study. She emphasized that sometimes students—in this case, undergraduates—offer invaluable assistance:

> There was some voice [i.e., an undergraduate's], and I hardly paid any attention. She [the student] said, "I think you might find this interesting, and I took it off a website—here it is." . . . So I read it . . . It was wonderful . . . I thought, "She has done more to educate me than my sort of wandering in the wilderness . . . just by presenting this material."

Through this brief though substantively important interaction, the undergraduate student and the mature scholar initiated a longer research collaboration, one in which the two learned from each other. Their ability to work together represents an instance of teaching, mentoring, research, and possibly outreach as happening simultaneously.

To summarize, we might view Elizabeth's teaching and research as united through a "mirror effect" of sorts: Her research is reflected in her teaching, and conversely, the content of her teaching and work with students is reflected in her research. Through this mirror effect, teaching and research support each other. As we have seen, Elizabeth sometimes draws outreach into the mix as well. Elizabeth, then, assumes agency by integrating purposefully many of her career responsibilities—multitasking in a sense, positioning one aspect of her work as a resource for another, braiding connections among strands of work such that they meld around subject matter. In Elizabeth's experience, research, teaching, and outreach are intertwined. She enacts, then, a strategy of the crafted career—a purposeful and careful selecting, shaping, and joining that, over time, blend the variety of activity that makes up her career.

In closing, we note that the integrative quality of Elizabeth's career does not come cleanly and clearly to her or to others like her. Her area of study is valued by her university, and thus she is advantaged, yet it is also clear that she actively works at her career, at times moving forward, at others retracing her steps. We might say that in addition to "landscaping" her career—selecting and planting within it, over time, activities that make sense side by side—that often she must weed and discard. Elizabeth, for example, found herself involved in a time-intensive governance activity that, in the end, could make no headway, given the lack of institutional support. Though having invested extended time in the effort, Elizabeth realized that she had to withdraw from it, in order to pursue the full expanse of her work. Elizabeth Ferrara, then, illustrates a strategy of integration and focus that she achieves by attending to her subjects of study across multiple work domains.

Strategy 2: Narrowing One's Scholarly Work So It Can Be Managed, Yet Ensuring That in Its Restricted Form it Retains Substance to be Learned

Newly tenured professors may rethink and reorganize their work to continue in their scholarly learning as they take on new senior-level responsibilities in service, teaching, and research. Faced with increased opportunities and obligations, Elizabeth Ferrara organizes her posttenure work in this way: She conceptualizes her scholarly learning clearly and uses it to define and bind her research, teaching, and outreach. Although she engages in different kinds of learning within each of these activities, her agenda for learning—*what* she struggles to learn—coheres across them all. In sum, Elizabeth strives to convert as many of her professional responsibilities as possible into sites for this scholarly learning, thereby binding disparate activities into a meaningful whole.

Another approach for maintaining one's agenda for scholarly learning, consistent with but different from Elizabeth's, is to narrow it: to restrict purposefully one's program of scholarly learning, though importantly, in ways that do not constrain its thoughtful development. The resulting agenda for scholarly learning must be substantial enough to be termed as "developing" and "advancing," yet not so cumbersome as to stall amid the growing array of posttenure work. A professor pursuing this course of action would be advised as follows: Mindfully chip away at the substantive breadth of your scholarly learning, especially in research, with an eye to maintaining its substantive development. A scholar who uses this strategy strives to preserve her scholarly learning by restricting its deviation from a defined core of ideas and tasks, but without constricting their meaningful growth. In doing so, the scholar adheres to a strategy of mindful containment.

As the next case suggests, a scholar who uses this strategy limits how he or she expends time and energy on scholarly learning, especially so in the context of research. One way to do this is to craft an agenda for scholarly learning that builds on one's past research-based learning, as long as that learning promises more. Such continuity may be substantive, perspectival, and/or methodological. What does a strategy of mindful containment offer?

Containment can buffer a scholar from disruptive discontinuities in thought requiring time and energy—for perspectival redefinition, methodological reconstruction, or substantive rebuilding—when such disruptions are *not* central to, or necessary for, that person's intellectual project. "Rework" of this sort—however rewarding—may detract from time otherwise devoted to the particular strand of learning a scholar is most deeply committed to. Such rework may also reduce attention to service, teaching, and advising—and to one's learning of them—an option that may not be viable under certain institutional conditions. Containment, then, calls on researchers to balance, thoughtfully and pragmatically, the new learning that disrupted understanding requires and the continued learning that containment, as a purposeful strategy, assumes.

Mindful containment, as a strategy for scholarly learning, resonates with Baltes and Baltes's (1990) conception of lifetime adaptation, and features "selection" and "optimization" as aspects of later-life cognition.[3] "Selection" refers to acts of intensified "restriction of one's life world to fewer domains of functioning" (eliminating the peripheral), with increasing attention, through time, to "domains that are of high priority" (attending to the valuable and central; p. 21). High-priority domains may be continuous over time, in the sense of *extension* that reflects little change, or they may be continuous yet transformed or otherwise "optimized" in the sense of *developmental change*.

We may apply this imagery to scholarly learning as follows: Over time, a professor's scholarly learning may become focused on a particular topic, perspective, or method (Baltes and Baltes's conception of "selection"), and the professor's work may move forward, though with little change to it, thus in the spirit of *extension*. For example, extension may occur as a scholar represents her or his early learning in new ways to diverse audiences. Such learning represents *extension* if little happens to the content of the scholar's learning over time, even if "research" is at play. Yet if learning content does change in substantial ways (becoming "optimized")—whether in the context of teaching, research, service, or outreach—then the change is *developmental*. Thus, although a professor's scholarly learning may become increasingly focused over time (for example, settling on a selected topic, perspective, method, etc.), it may nonetheless change substantially (become "optimized"), for example, as that professor comes to understand the subjects in different ways, though within a tighter frame; this change is *developmental*. Despite this developmental possibility, containment, as a strategy, does pose

risks—for professors, perhaps an overattachment to a particular subject, perspective, or method that, in obviating alternatives, overly narrows the range
of what may be learned. "Selection" and "optimization" require mindful
attention for learning to proceed.

We offer excerpts from interviews with Benjamin Lucas, a recently tenured social scientist, as he describes how and why he applies a strategy of
containment to his scholarly learning. We attend especially to his watchfulness over the strategy's narrowing effects: He needs to narrow the range of
his scholarship to make his workload manageable, yet he worries that exces-
sive narrowing will stifle the developmental features of his work.

Benjamin comes across as serious, even solemn, as hard working and
pragmatic. A humorous turn, however, periodically sneaks through an otherwise grave and businesslike demeanor, and an occasional laugh comes as a
surprise.

The greatest change in Benjamin's posttenure work life has been a sharp
increase in administrative responsibilities. Asked at what point his service
load increased, he says:

> I wouldn't say that it went up. I would say that it landed like a piano on
> my back about a year after I got tenure. . . . After the promotion, I was
> asked to serve on a series of committees, some more enjoyable and produc-
> tive than others. But a huge number. And didn't feel that I was in a posi-
> tion to say no.

In both interviews, but especially in the second, Benjamin detailed the
challenges he faced in balancing his research commitments and emerging
service and administrative responsibilities:

> I find that I'm a little bit more frustrated trying to get stuff done now than
> I was previously. Because I had had very few administrative responsibilities
> [then, before tenure]. Even right after having gotten tenure. But since then,
> I'm . . . on far too many committees to even be able to remember which
> specific ones I'm on. And I'm also the director of [an academic program],
> so that eats up a substantial amount of otherwise productive research time.
> So I think it's been increasingly difficult to balance the research with the
> administrative part of it. The teaching is less of a burden because the ad-
> ministrative responsibilities bought out some of my teaching time. But I
> find that it's harder to combine the research with the administration than

it is to combine the research with the teaching . . . the administrative stuff, it seems to always be a new crisis that comes up every, every . . . week or couple of weeks. And then endless meetings . . . and cases drag on to no productive end. So I think if anything, that's the biggest change over the last couple years, the difficulty to balancing those two. It's gotten a little bit easier in the last year or so because there was a fairly steep learning curve, particularly [my being] in this position as director of [the academic program]. [Predecessors in the role] didn't keep really detailed records. . . . And as a consequence, there were a lot of things that needed to be done from scratch.

Through his early posttenure career, Benjamin has been learning about institutional service, its management, and the organizational terrains that give it form. He has also worked hard to maintain and develop his research. But unlike Elizabeth Ferrara, he has been challenged in connecting these two prominent streams of his work. As he says, he finds it "increasingly difficult to balance the research with the administra[tion]" because of differences in their content. The research represents continuity with his past work focused on a large-scale social phenomenon; his growing administrative and service responsibilities, on the other hand, require his attentiveness to crisis after crisis in his workplace, and none relate neatly to the content of his research. These are two disparate, nonintegrative streams of effort, each entailing tasks of *doing* and of *learning to do*. As he also points out, creating overlaps between his teaching and research as a strategy for advancing learning across the two is not viable, since his administrative position comes with "teaching buyouts" which, his colleagues anticipate, should free up his time for service. Paradoxically, this "release time" from teaching may accentuate the contrast in his work life between the content of his service, which he has to both learn and do, and the content of his research. Benjamin's case suggests the following: When service fails to support research (because of the absence of a substantive connection between them), and when teaching falls out of the work equation, then service and research are likely to clash. They separate and compete for a professor's time, attention, and energy.

Given this predicament, a strategy of integration, like Elizabeth Ferrara's, is less helpful to Benjamin Lucas than a strategy of containment, defined as the purposeful narrowing of one's research to its core of meaning, coupled, however, with watchfulness so that meaningful restriction does not turn into stifling constriction.[4] Benjamin describes his worries in this regard:

I'm concerned sometimes that I've become like a person who's got a particularly good hammer for whom every problem looks like a nail. And you wind up finding new ways of using this particular technique or this particular perspective, and that shapes your research in a way that I don't remember having seen my research shaped before. . . . . So I've been doing this [using a particular perspective and related research method] in looking at [topic]. I've been doing it for [another topic] and have actually gotten three . . . papers now written that use this, the same basic set-up. The problem is there's a big investment in learning how to do this, and the programming is difficult, and getting it to work with the statistics is often difficult. And it's often difficult to explain to audiences that aren't familiar with it. So you've invested all this time and effort in the technique, and then you wind up looking for ways of applying it, rather than for necessarily identifying an interesting question, and think what's the appropriate technique . . . to use in this circumstance. So that's the sense in which I'm a little bit uneasy about this particular turning point in my career. So I'm not, I'm not sure I'm as . . . capable of learning new tricks as I was when I was fifteen years junior to where I am now. . . . It took me a while to be able to assimilate this technique, and I think it took me longer than it would have if I was still in graduate school and not as set in the ways of doing what I've been doing. So it was difficult to learn how to do it. . . . [But] now I think I've probably spent too much time using it. So it makes me a feel a little bit uncomfortable sometimes.

Benjamin makes an important point in this interview. We hear that as a young scholar, he learned broadly and that from this learning, he "assimilated" a "technique" (a research method) that continues even now to guide his research. Though appreciating the utility of this method for his research, including the scholarly success it has brought him, Benjamin worries about what its overuse may do to his work over time and subsequently, we might gather, to the knowledge that constitutes his field. "And you wind up finding new ways of using this particular technique or this particular perspective," he says, "and that shapes your research in a way that I don't remember having seen my research shaped before." In applying this method consistently, a function of what we might call methodological (and possibly perspectival) "selection" (per Baltes & Baltes, 1990), Benjamin obviates the need for alternative routes that might open up his thoughts and his inquiry generally. Research methods do guide, but used uncritically, they may restrict to the point of constriction. Yet Benjamin worries that he no longer has the time or energy to move back to his pre-"selection" days ("I'm not sure I'm as . . . capable of learning new tricks as I was when I was fifteen years junior to where I am now"). Second, we hear in Benjamin's statement, an uneasiness and sense of being uncomfortable intellectually as he walks a fine line in his early posttenure career between a view of research as *extension* (extending methods, perspectives, and knowledge from the past into the future with little substantive change to them) and a view of research as *development* (an extension of one's past learning that nonetheless grows and evolves from within itself, becoming internally transformed, through new meaning).

The case of Benjamin Lucas and his career-crafting strategy leaves us with feelings of unease as we share in his anxiety of what it means to walk a tightrope between *extension* and *development* in scholarly work. Though his future cannot be assured, we may nonetheless find hope in the consistent awareness and wide-awake reflectiveness Benjamin engages in. He does not deny the risk of stalled learning but, rather, faces it—uneasily, with discomfort as he says—but openly. We suggest that this courageous openness to risk (in this case, of failure) along with the discomfort (and, we suggest, fear) it provokes, gives Benjamin reason to stay alive in his learning: Benajmin's discomfort, in fact, serves as a wakeup call, alerting him to the risks of the overly narrowed learning that a strategy of containment provokes, but also, then, to opportunities for exceeding these risks. He therefore augments his strategy of containment with one of watchful venturesomeness:

> I: Do you know a lot of other people who are [in this position, using a containment strategy]? I mean, I guess one thing I'm hearing from you is that you're aware of that.
>
> BL: Yes . . . I know lots of other people who do exactly the same, the same thing. . . . they'll develop a new . . . technique, and they'll spend the rest of their career looking for places to apply it. I'm not so interested in the technique. I'm interested in asking and answering interesting questions, and I'm just concerned that the range of questions that I can plausibly address has been substantially reduced by focusing on a particular technique. So fortunately, the stuff I'm doing on [new topic of research], there's no need to do that [i.e., use again the same perspective/ method]. . . . It's a completely . . . different set of issues, and a different approach that I can use for that. So being able to do that research now has made me a little bit less uncomfortable than I had been previously.

Within his early posttenure career, Benjamin learns how to continue his research within bounds, yet he also develops strategies for its refreshment—or for avoiding its stagnation. He learns how to open up new possibilities for scholarly learning within manageable limits.

We came to view Benjamin as desiring to grow in his research-based thinking, but also to contain it, sensibly, to allow time for his other work (including learning it). He tempered his research containment strategy with watchfulness, initially to avoid overcommitment, and later to make room for new commitments that might refresh his research. His enacted strategy responds then to his above-all need to manage his scholarly learning in ways that preserve its continuance, its integrity, and not least, the promise of its development. A strategy of containment, mindfully applied, helps make this possible. While we cannot discern Benjamin's future, this strategy of containing scholarly learning within "small places," promises, paradoxically, the possibility of its growth in future years. If this happens, Benjamin will need to decide in the future how to engage in space-expansion strategies for his learning. We suggest this may be an aim of his later career.

Strategy 3: Creating Orderly Environments That Promote Resourcefulness and Self-Sufficiency, Thereby Limiting Distractions and Conserving Reserves of Personal Energy and Time for Scholarly Learning

Professors in this study displayed another noteworthy strategy: creating infrastructures that limit the spend-down of energy and time reserves, freeing these up for professors' scholarly learning. However, we present it with a caveat: that a professor may claim this strategy as supportive of scholarly learning only if devoting comparable effort to the learning itself, and then, only if it is clear that the professor can house scholarly efforts in the structures the professor clears and creates. Though entailing "the clearing of a space and cleaning it up," this strategy also involves stage setting: creating by design environments that fit and support the narratives of scholarly learning that a scholar and the scholar's colleagues will enact, even if narrative content cannot be foretold.

How might we know this strategy when we see it? Professors use this strategy to help hold at bay distracting forces that, uncontrolled, may deplete energy for scholarly study. This strategy supports scholarly learning in less direct ways than the preceding two: by clearing a space and setting the stage for it, along with the day-to-day work that must go on around it. Inspired by Baltes and Baltes's (1990) vision of agency as involving adults who create "ecologies that, in addition to providing development-enhancing conditions, are less taxing on [those] persons' reserve capacities" (p. 20), we note that study participants assume agency in one of two ways: directly (reflected in the two preceding strategies), and indirectly. Newly tenured professors relying on *indirection* often use their mounting service and administrative responsibilities to create workplaces where they can craft strategies, like those of Elizabeth and Benjamin, allowing them to edge as close as they can to their preferred learning; as a strategy, this third approach is, then, rudimentary. It offers few *direct* benefits to strategists, and may be viewed instead as a ground-clearing investment that may or may not pan out. Professor Carmen Elias-Jones's efforts to clear and rebuild the academic programs she coordinates exemplify this well: Carmen reconstructs work settings that in due time, and if all goes well, may allow her reengagement in scholarly work.

Carmen is a musician, teacher, and performer devoted to creating musical sound. In year 1 of the study, expressions of vivid "passionate thought" filled her interview:

> CE: But it is really the issue of . . . listening to music, and really listening to it, I think, . . . as a musician, in a different way than most people would. It is like you are inside it and living it, and it moves you across a gamut of emotions. Then, there's the actual act of playing, and because there is a certain amount of naturalness, I think that will happen. . . . But the actual act of playing, when there is naturalness about it, it is very hard to explain . . . it is almost like—it is a thrill, it is a huge thrill, you know, really . . . like a complete focus of oneness, you know, with the instrument. And then you can hear yourself producing [this] thing that moves you so. It is, it is a challenge and a reward—all at the same time on so many different levels.
>
> I: You said [that] first you were in it and then you are actually making it.
>
> CE: Yeah. You are actually making it, yeah. And then . . . physically, I mean you spend so much time physically actually with the instrument, and being able to conquer it, and then hear this—, and it is a good sound, you know . . . a good sound. I don't think there is anything that equals that feeling. And being able to do it . . . sometimes it is really, it is fun. . . . There is a whole, it is [a] big physical thrill. You know, feeling the [instrument] and that when you change how you play, you

get a different sound. And the different sound makes you feel a different way.

In her first interview, Carmen focuses almost exclusively on her creative efforts: Her "work" at this time *is* her creative effort. "I'm a musician," she says, "and that's not really work." Asked whether her current work situation at the university supports development of "really deep . . . experiences with music," she replies, "The work situation does support creative activity. . . . We really are left very much to our own devices." Amid her music, Carmen teaches in many one-to-one sessions daily. She also coordinates a small undergraduate music program, as she has for years. However Carmen says little about this work in the first interview. She talks mostly of her music.

In her second interview two and a half years later, Carmen tells us she has gained management responsibility for a second program, larger and more complex than the one she had mentioned briefly in year 1. With the increased service, Carmen's life—the life of her mind—has changed. Asked whether her creative work had changed over the preceding two years, she says:

> No, not necessarily. I find that I have a harder time, I had a harder time, somewhere in the middle of the past two or three years, I had a harder time trying to juggle my time. Trying to find the good time for my practicing and thinking about me. I found myself being spread very thin. I found myself being extremely frantic. And so I would say that in some ways [this] is a low point. . . . It was partly because of all the administrative duties, and my not being shrewd enough and savvy enough, having really come from the fearful days of saying yes to everything, and at whatever the cost to myself or to my time. So that was . . . really, I would say, a low point, a very hectic point.

Within a few years of her tenure award, Carmen, like others in her cohort, experienced an expansion of institutional service responsibilities. She tells us, in year 3 of the study, that the added work marks "a low point" in her life and career, since it cuts into time for music and "thinking about me . . . being spread very thin . . . being extremely frantic."

At a point like this, a scholar might strive to distance herself from program service, to learn to say "no" assertively, and focus on core creative or scholarly work. Yet, Carmen takes a different tack. Rather than resisting the call to program service, she addresses it openly and aggressively, in fact, rede-fining it in ways that, over time, she hopes will support her scholarly work. How? Carmen dutifully and aggressively takes on the enlarged program co-ordination responsibilities foisted on her. For example, she revises program functioning around a software package that enhances person-to-person and programwide communication. In doing so, she reorganizes the program's in-frastructure to align it with her aspirations to create space and time for music. "I grew from that," she tells us in retrospect, "and learned how to find efficient ways to do things." Rather than shirking new responsibilities, Carmen takes them on seriously, shaping them and shaping also the systems of work they entail in ways that, as she sees it, promise to get her back to the work she most loves, her music:

> CE: [I found some] very essential ways of conveying information, using technology. Not because I'm a technology fiend but because I think that . . . there is something to be said for just being efficient about it. Whatever aspersions are cast on me for being a fiend about . . . commu-nication, it frees me up really to have time. . . . It's not time, I'm an efficient person, but it's just to have the energy, the quality sort of en-ergy to let my mind roam, and to think up projects and think of what I want do next. . . . So in a way, has it changed? I don't know. I mean, I wasn't really conscious of the change. I was conscious of bad, bad times, struggling. But I think that I have come to a point where it has become easier.
>
> I: Okay. If I could ask a couple of questions. First of all, the administrative duties, you're referring to the coordination . . . What's involved in that for you, the coordination?
>
> CE: Well, it's, it, everything that really has to do with [music classifica-tion]. All the scheduling, the academic curriculum . . . and also some balancing [of] the nitty gritty . . . the academic grind of the calendar, and of being fair and taking care of next year's incoming class. I mean, we have hundreds of applications per year out of which we pick, you know, [less than a dozen] . . . And so, you know, that itself [is hard]. But then added to that is a sense of vision. You know, so that we can create an academic environment that's exciting. It's not just the grind of the academic calendar, but new initiatives [that] are exciting. So in fact, you know, this past year . . . we had, for the first time, a new [activity] . . . to get it going for the first time, and, you know, to balance all the politics, and not offending people. And yet, trying to make sure

that it's "a go" was at once stressful and yet also very exciting, while it is happening . . . Trying to get sort of, you know, realizing my program is the only one that doesn't have full fellowships. And suddenly thinking to myself, "Why shouldn't we have them?" So I said, "Well, I have a brilliant idea . . . let's ask for them." And you know, it's not so easy, as you know . . . asking for something, and you have to balance all that. So trying to balance the two was always difficult because underneath, the real energy-sapping stuff is the tedious stuff. But . . . I'm proud to say I've gotten much better at it.

I: I'm curious of the sorts of things you do to make it better for you. . . . you mentioned using technology communication?

CE: Yeah. You know, you know, amongst the hats that I wear, I've . . . actually always been coordinator of [first program], [the coordination of the new program] is the other thing I do. . . . [When I started in this work] I wasn't even seeing these [kinds of musicians], and I had to take care of putting them in . . . groups. And they would complain. I mean, I'd come in here, and my message machine would just be blinking. And I think, to this day, I'm not over the fear that comes at seeing what messages are on my answering machine. Well, you know, they had, they had this wonderful thing that was developed at [name of developer]. . . . [And] I thought, "If I could just have some way of doing all this electronically . . . [have] some way for the kids to contact each other, for them to chat [with] each other, to make a kind of communication system." Because [given the physical layout of the program] the students don't see one another. We don't see our cohorts in some of the other programs or departments. And so I wanted, I wanted everything to be done on-line. I wanted it to be a form of communication. [Discusses the software that she discovered that could facilitate these efforts.] And so I went for a training session, actually in the middle of a very busy week. But when my graduate assistant told me about this [software program], I was extremely excited. I mean, he thought I was nuts. So I went for the training and I just thought, "This is exactly what we want." So I persuaded the other [program] coordinators . . . that we had to do this. And now, we are completely electronic. There are thousands of hits on the site. We send out mass mailings. My nuisance phone calls have been cut down almost 100 fold. . . . Everything is done electronically, everything is just, you know, I don't answer phone calls when I get them. . . . Everything is done like that, so I was so taken by that. I now do it, I developed a site just for [type of music], the whole . . .

> program, so I tried to persuade my [coordinator] colleagues to use it.
> . . . I made little folders for them, I gave them a little training session.
> I said, "Really, it's not that difficult. I can do it, you can do it, too."
> . . . And so . . . I have to say I keep recommending that [software]
> program. And it's not because I love that on its own, but [that] it is a
> tool to get rid of the tedium.

To help manage program resources and activities, directing them at interested persons, and thereby shifting distracting requests (for example, for information) away from herself, Carmen adopted an electronic platform that, in her words, helped "to get rid of the tedium" that would otherwise have pervaded her work life. The platform reduced her involvement in programwide conversations unrelated to her own work in music. It thereby released Carmen to attend to other thoughts, the scholarly among them, while connecting students and faculty to program resources.

Carmen's strategy—to adopt an electronic platform for program management—allows her to conserve what Baltes and Baltes (1990) might call her "reserve capacity," namely latent energy she can devote to music rather than program management. The program management system that Carmen installs helps her create an "optimizing environment . . . [an] ecolog[y] that, in addition to providing development-enhancing conditions, [is] less taxing on [a] person's reserve capacities" (p. 20). In adopting this strategy, Carmen clears space in her work life for creative pursuit. She thereby creates a work environment that promises to free her to attend to her artistic and scholarly work with music, thereby facilitating her development as a musician.

Closing Thoughts: Agency and Strategic Response, Learning, and Professors' Careers

The narratives of Elizabeth Ferrara, Benjamin Lucas, and Carmen Elias-Jones portray three strategic responses to a learning dilemma of the early posttenure career: how to navigate between (a) an internal call to learning, in scholarship, that responds to questions of personal meaning in professors' lives (Neumann & Peterson, 1997); and (b) an external call to learning that responds to others' needs, and to which tenured professors may feel compelled to respond. The external call involves learning to carry out teaching, service, research, or outreach tasks that have little bearing on one's committed interests.[5] But why struggle to navigate between these two "calls to learn" when commitment to one or the other would be clearer?

We believe it important to create a career that navigates between these two calls for two reasons: First, current research indicates that professors' engagement in personally meaningful work is related to their intellectual vitality—the substantive energy that propels their scholarly efforts (Neumann, 1999a, 1999b; Neumann & Peterson, 1997; Neumann, 2005). Second, in light of concerns about institutional survival and/or advancement, university leaders call increasingly for faculty contributions to institution-building efforts, whether through research, teaching, outreach, or service. As recent recipients of the "gift" of lifetime tenure, those newly tenured may be especially vulnerable to such calls. And indeed, they are, especially within the expanding service domain of their work (Neumann, 1999c; Neumann & Terosky, 2003). It is of course hard, questionable, and unwise for a professor to shirk calls for that professor's skills and expertise in an increasingly service-oriented and accountability driven work environment, or to be nonresponsive within peer professional relationships and cultures of colleagueship, which by virtue of tenure must last a lifetime (Neumann, 2000; Smelser, 1993) . Yet often, professors' service-oriented or responsibility-driven work, however important to others, distances them from the personal research interests that may surface as well at this career stage. How to attend to both, or navigate between them, without compromising the integrity and quality of either—and how to learn, through deep engagement in each, what "good work" entails—is the question at issue.

We learn, in this chapter, that there is more than one way to address this question. Drawing on the words of participants in a study of learning and development in the early posttenure career, we present three distinct responses framed as *strategy*. Elizabeth Ferrara integrates several very different career activities (research, outreach, teaching/mentoring) around a substantive core, the subject of study she cares for deeply and pursues consistently. She struggles for coherence—a sense of common purpose—across disparate professional activities. To do so, she positions her work in one domain of her job, as a professor, to support and advance work in other domains (rather than treating separate work domains as though they were separate jobs, each requiring different thought and energy). We might term her navigational strategy as *putting it together*. Benjamin Lucas addresses the challenge of "navigation without compromise" by thoughtfully narrowing his research—

that is, restricting its range but maintaining enough breadth in substance and method to allow meaningful contribution to his field. His strategy—the mindful containment of his research-based learning—allows Benjamin to learn on the job, to learn how to carry out his new program coordination responsibilities while maintaining his scholarship. We might entitle his navigational strategy as *learning to learn, in ever increasing ways, in shrinking intellectual spaces.* Carmen Elias-Jones takes an altogether different approach to navigating between the work that, organizationally, she feels compelled to do and the work that her artistry demands. Carmen chooses to devote substantial time to revamping her work environment to make it conducive to work so that through time she (and others too) can build into it. By turning her new posttenure service obligations (program coordination) into opportunities to redefine her workplace—building expectations of and possibilities for resourcefulness and self-sufficiency into it—she minimizes distractions to work she cares about. Carmen thereby defines a work space that allows her—and, no doubt, others too—to engage in personally meaningful work. She invokes, by design, the ecology of her future scholarly and creative efforts, thereby, creating "space" for her future work. We might term Carmen's navigational strategy as *invoking design.*

Although these cases may serve as guides for strategic response, we append two caveats. First, these strategies should *not* be viewed as the be-all and end-all of what it takes to create a successful tenured career. Professors may need to bring other strategies into play, whether as variations on or departures from those presented here. What seems important is simply having a strategy, with the understanding that strategic content is likely to vary relative to the person and situation. Second, professors would likely benefit from assessing regularly their strategies-in-use and redirecting them as warranted. Unconscious and unassessed strategy—or agency accepted uncritically—may become misguided.

Drawing on the cases of Elizabeth Ferrara, Benjamin Lucas, and Carmen Elias-Jones, we conclude with the following observations on agency, strategy, and learning in professors' careers, as well as related questions for future research:

First, though institutional standards, needs, and expectations do, of necessity, influence the work content of professors' careers, professors *can* assume initiative in the substantive crafting of their careers: *what* they study and otherwise learn, *what* research they pursue, *what* the content of their teaching, outreach, and service is. This observation suggests the following questions for future research: What features of institutional and collegial life shape the substance of professors' careers? How aware are professors of such shaping? How and to what extent do professors respond to it? To what extent are they able to identify, within campus life, cultural resources for their preferred work? What facilitates such identification? How may professors address, productively, the absence of resources critical to their efforts to learn in meaningful ways?

Second, agency need not be viewed as privileging personal-professorial over institutional interests, or as antithetical to adaptivity (responsiveness to institutional needs) within academic work. The cases herein presented in no way suggest that professors, attentive to the personal meaning of their work, are irresponsible or unresponsive to their larger communities. Rather the cases show it is possible for professors to respond, reasonably, to external calls for their labor, and simultaneously to persist in scholarly study that matters in their lives. This observation suggests the following research questions: Beyond the strategies that Elizabeth, Benjamin, and Carmen use to manage their learning, what others may professors employ? Which strategies work well, and under what conditions? How might professors become aware of these, and use them fruitfully?

Third, developing agency requires time and effort. It requires thought, reflection, learning through trial and error, creativity, continuing assessment, and, no doubt, persistence and courage. Such effort wisely invested promises to pay off: When we last met, Elizabeth described a scholarly agenda that was up and running, Benjamin laid out a plan of new research even as he spoke of struggles with his service load, and Carmen described how her administrative reforms would, in due time, likely garner time for her career. Since we did not follow these scholars beyond the third project year, we cannot, conclusively, report happy endings, yet we can report on their navigational progress, along with the hope, optimism, and resolve that their progress prompted. This observation suggests the following questions: How might professors build time for strategizing and for developing agency— across research, teaching, service, and outreach—into their work lives? What help do they need to do so in ways that honor, emphatically, desires to bridge the two calls to learn that this chapter highlights? How might such strategizing unfold within an academic life, given that strategy making, like learning, may need to be timed for developmental appropriateness?

Fourth, though higher-education writers and researchers typically refer to service in organizational terms, they should explore it, too, as a strand of the academic career, and thus, as a personal-professional task to be learned and strategized thoughtfully. As with teaching, service involves knowledge and skill that few doctoral students develop prior to assuming assistant professorships, and that few understand prior to accession to tenure (Neumann & Terosky, 2003). As with teaching, too, most do not "take seriously" (see Terosky, 2005) the service strand of their careers until by virtue of its full-blown presence in their work lives, they must. This observation suggests these research questions: Given the unique resources and constraints of the disciplinary knowledge at issue, how may professors conceptualize their service obligations as contributing usefully to their scholarly careers? What might it mean to "take seriously" one's service obligations in careers committed to scholarly learning?

Fifth, it is known that the service loads of academic women and members of underrepresented minorities can be unreasonably high (Turner & Myers, 1999). We worry, further, that the service of some may not link well with their teaching and research. A high service load that is decoupled from other "core" responsibilities, and the absence of a guiding frame for scholarly learning, may in the long run yield but splintered and partial "products." We know, only too well, that the kind of positive work integration that Elizabeth Ferrara portrays is not shared by all professors. This observation yields the following research questions: How is integration, as a feature of faculty work, represented demographically across the faculty? What differences exist relative to gender, ethnicity, age (within rank), and other features of faculty background? What differences exist relative to field and institution? What explains the differences? Given that faculty are not born knowing how to integrate the work they encounter on the job, and in fact that they have to learn how to do this, we also ask: How accessible is such learning to all faculty? How equitably are opportunities for work integration distributed across a faculty? In raising these questions, we must note the tenuous—though indeed, courageous—aspects of Carmen Elias-Jones's strategy: Carmen's approach is, perhaps, all too familiar to academic women and other faculty who come to be saddled with program housekeeping chores that seem never to cease, that are substantially "other-directed," and that "promote" their incumbents into ever more challenging cleanup roles under the guise of assumed leadership. How might we distinguish, within academic service and leadership, roles that entail "unending housework" from others that are more creative and fulfilling? How are these very different roles shared across divisions of gender, ethnicity, class, and other aspects of personal background?

Sixth, scholarly learning—as a feature of professors' research and teaching, and occasionally of their outreach and service—seems more prominent in some professors' lives than others. And it may be more prominent in the mentoring of some professors than others. Scholarly learning also may be valued and supported in some institutional cultures more than in others. Research questions that grow out of this observation are as follows: How do professors whose careers involve extended engagement in scholarly learning—within any aspect of their work—craft their careers? How do they learn to be professors? How do colleagues, institutions, or other sources support them? Who among the faculty needs improved access to such sources? How might such access be provided?

We hope this chapter will spur attention to the importance of agency, strategy, and learning in professors' posttenure career development. Though these concepts are unlikely to settle concerns about what it takes to support professors desiring to maintain or reignite their intellectual and professional vitality throughout their careers, we hope they will provide openings for further inquiry.

References

Baltes, P. B., & Baltes, M. M. (1990). *Successful aging: Perspectives from the behavioral sciences*. New York: Cambridge University Press.

Berger, P., & Luckmann, T. (1966). *The social construction of reality: A treatise in the sociology of knowledge*. Garden City, NY: Doubleday.

Bourdieu, P. (1986). The forms of capital. In J. G. Richardson (Ed.), *Handbook of theory and research for the sociology of education*. New York: Greenwood Press.

Buchmann, M. (1989). *The script of life in modern society: Entry into adulthood in a changing world*. Chicago: University of Chicago Press.

Clausen, J. (1991). Adolescent competence and the shaping of the life course. *American Journal of Sociology, 96*, 805–842.

Dannefer, D., & Perlmutter, M. (1990). Development as a multidimensional process: Individual and social constituents. *Human Development, 33*, 108–137.

Elder, G. H. (1994). Time, human agency, and social change: Perspectives on the life course. *Social Psychology Quarterly, 57*(1), 4–15.

Elder, G. H. (1997). The life course and human development. In W. Damon & R. M. Lerner (Eds.), *Handbook of Child Psychology* (5th ed., pp. 939–991). New York: Wiley.

Elder, G. H. (1999). *Children of the great depression: Social change in life experiences.* Boulder, CO: Westview.

Glaser, B., & Strauss, A. (1967). *The discovery of grounded theory: Strategies for qualitative research.* New York: Aldine.

Kerr, C. (1995). *The uses of the university.* Cambridge, MA: Harvard University Press.

Lerner, R., & Busch-Rossnagel, N. (1981). Individuals as procedures of their development: Conceptual and empirical bases. In R. Lerner & N. Busch-Rossnagel (Eds.), *Individuals as producers of their development: A life-span perspective* (pp. 1–36). New York: Cambridge University Press.

Marshall, V. (2000). *Agency, structure and the life course in the era of reflexive modernization.* Paper presented at the annual meeting of the American Sociological Association, Washington, DC.

Mayer, K. U., & Schoepflin, U. (1989). The state and the life course. *Annual Review of Sociology, 15,* 187–209.

Neugarten, B., Moore, J. W., & Lowe, J. C. (1965). Age norms, age constraints, and adult socialization. *American Journal of Sociology, 70,* 710–717.

Neumann, A. (1999a). Inventing a labor of love: Scholarship as a woman's work. In M. Romero & A. J. Stewart (Eds.), *Women's untold stories: Breaking silence, talking back, voicing complexity* (pp. 243–255). New York: Routledge.

Neumann, A. (1999b, April). *Professing passion: Views of passionate thought in scholarship.* Paper presented at the annual meeting of the American Educational Research Association, Montreal, Canada.

Neumann, A. (1999c). *Between the work I love and the work I do: Creating professors and scholars in the early post-tenure career* (Occasional Paper Series, Paper No. 57). Ann Arbor, Michigan: University of Michigan, Center for the Education of Women, Institute for Research on Women and Gender.

Neumann, A. (2000). Helping to foster collegiality for newcomers. In E. M. Bensimon, K. Ward, & K. Sanders (Eds.), *The department chair's role in developing new faculty into teachers and scholars* (pp. 123–125). Bolton, MA: Anker.

Neumann, A. (2005). To glimpse beauty and awaken meaning: Scholarly learning as aesthetic experience. *Journal of Aesthetic Education, 39*(4), 68–88.

Neumann, A., & Peterson, P. L. (1997). *Learning from our lives: Women, research, and autobiography in education.* New York: Teachers College Press.

Neumann, A., & Terosky, A. L. (2003). *Toward images of reciprocity in faculty service: Insights from a study of the earlier post-tenure career.* Paper presented at the annual meeting of the American Educational Research Association, Chicago.

O'Rand, A. (1996). The precious and the precocious: Understanding cumulative disadvantage and cumulative advantage over the life course. *Gerontologist, 26*, 230–238.

O'Rand, A. (2000). Structuration and individualization: The life course as a continuous, multilevel process. In A. C. Kerckhoff (Ed.), *Generating social stratification: Towards a new research agenda* (pp. 1–16). Boulder, CO: Westview.

Schatzman, L., and Strauss, A. L., (1973). *Field research: Strategies for a natural Sociology*. New Jersey: Prentice-Hall.

Schutz, A. (1970). *The phenomenology of the social world* (H. R. Wagner, Trans.). Chicago: University of Chicago Press.

Smelser, N. J. (1993). *Effective committee service*. Newbury Park, CA: Sage.

Sorensen, A. (1986). Social structure and mechanisms of life course processes. In A. B. Sorenson, F. E. Weinert, & L. R. Sherrod (Eds.), *Human development and the life course* (pp. 177–198). Hillsdale, NJ: Erlbaum.

Terosky, A. L. (2005). *Taking teaching seriously: A study of university professors and their undergraduate teaching*. Unpublished doctoral dissertation, Teachers College, Columbia University, New York.

Tierney, W. G., & Bensimon, E. M. (1996). *Promotion and tenure: Community and socialization in academe*. Albany, NY: SUNY Press.

Turner, C. S. V., & Myers, S. L. (1999). *Faculty of color in academe: Bittersweet success*. Essex, UK: Pearson Education.

Weick, K. (1979). *The social psychology of organizing*. Reading, MA: Addison-Wesley.

Notes

1. However, agency and learning fail to overlap in some ways. For example, the social content of learning, and skepticism as an element of inquiry-oriented learning, are more apparent in learning than in agency.

2. To comply with pledges of confidentiality, we name no institution or person, and we omit or mask potentially identifying data. Some professors requested that instead of indicating their specific disciplines or fields, that we use broader descriptors, for example, a biologist wishing to be called a scientist, or a political scientist wishing to be described as a social scientist.

3. Baltes and Baltes (1990) emphasize three aspects of lifetime adaptation, though with attention to older age: selection, optimization, and compensation. For the purposes of this chapter, we attend only to selection and optimization; compensation, though worthy of consideration, was less obvious through data review and bears attention for studies of the professoriate in later life.

4. As we discuss later, these strategies would, no doubt, benefit from connection to other strategies employed simultaneously, in this case, possibly, a strategy of rea-

sonable *service containment*. We discuss such strategies in Neumann and Terosky, 2003.

5. Such calls to learning are, no doubt, acceptable and important to carry out in a well-balanced work portfolio. A professor, like other workers, must occasionally do (and learn to do) work viewed as necessary though inconsistent with the professor's developing agenda and interests. Typically such work takes time and energy away from "core work" without giving much, directly, back to it. Examples include representation on a committee concerned with a topic of little interest to a professor, teaching a class that must be taught because of its centrality to a curriculum but that the professor would like to "give away," and so on. We by no means suggest that such necessary work be dropped from professors' workloads, as that is unrealistic. Yet in this chapter and in other works, we suggest that overengagement in work that is tangential to a professors' core interests—to the point of shutting those interests down or otherwise frustrating them—may be harmful to professors' intellectual vitality, potentially their greatest professional resource. Carmen Elias-Jones is a case in point: If her program "cleanup" tasks were to absorb her attention, distracting her from her core musical work for an inordinate period of time, we would view her situation as problematic; if she can carry out the cleanup work in a reasonable time frame, and turn then to her own work in a newly supportive environment, then this aspect of her work portfolio seems reasonable. This, of course, is also why Benjamin Lucas's commitment to maintaining a large enough window for his own scholarly work while running his program is important. In writing these statements, we note that in addition to addressing organizational work needs, a "balanced portfolio" must address, as well, the intellectual needs of the professor.

6

FACULTY CHANGE INITIATIVES
Responding to a Campus Climate Study

Jeni Hart

I n the late 1990s, a comprehensive study initiated by collective action among several faculty women in the School of Science at Massachusetts Institute of Technology (MIT) found disparities that favored male academics in salary, office and laboratory space, awards, resources, committee assignments, named chairs, teaching obligations, and institutional responses to outside job offers to retain faculty (MIT, 1999). With the support of their dean and president, the network of women made several recommendations: (a) ensure equity for senior women faculty, (b) improve the professional lives of junior women faculty, and (c) increase the number of women faculty (MIT, 1999). Their study witnessed some immediate institutional responses and received wide, national attention. In addition to this change at MIT, other institutions, including Rutgers University, the University of Michigan, and the University of California-Los Angeles (UCLA), were inspired to investigate inequities on their own campuses (National Academy of Sciences, 2004).

At Southwest University,[1] a study that became known as the Faculty Climate Project took up similar concerns. The project was entirely initiated by faculty leaders, representing a collaboration between the president of the Organization for Faculty Women (OFW) and the chair of the Commission on the Status of Women (CSW), with no charge or direction initiating from

Data gathering for this manuscript was supported by Rutgers University as part of the Re-affirming Action: Designs for Diversity in Higher Education, a grant funded by the Ford Foundation.

the university administration. The university administration did, however, provide the funding for the project after being approached by the Faculty Climate faculty leadership. *The Faculty Climate Project: Report in Detail* (Cress, 2001; Cress, Dinnerstein, Miller, & Hart, 2001), was released in October 2001.

The goals of the Faculty Climate Project were to measure the campus climate for faculty women and faculty of color. Over 270 faculty were interviewed and these data were triangulated with institutional data and survey results from a nationally normed faculty study in which over 800 Southwest faculty participated. The findings identified multiple aspects of the campus climate that must change in order to enhance academic excellence. Moreover, the report suggested that unless climate issues were addressed, the university's goal of achieving an academic environment that will allow all faculty, staff, and students to be productive and unhindered by any impediments because of gender, race/ethnicity, disability, sexual orientation, or any other reason would be compromised. Further, a subsequent study was conducted to complement the study of faculty at Southwest University and focused on university staff and their experiences of campus climate. *The Staff Climate Project: Phase II* (Johnsrud, Perreira, Miller, Inoshita, & Hart, 2002) was released in October, 2002.

Purpose of This Study

Although significant research has been carried out on the campus level to assess the campus climate for faculty (National Academy of Sciences, 2004), little has been done to investigate the impact of the findings of these studies. Southwest University was in a unique position to decide how to implement the recommendations to create a campus that was more diverse, hospitable, and fair. Moreover, its experiences might serve as an example of how these studies can move beyond just a report on a shelf to a living document that can transform a college or university. Specifically, the purpose of this study is to explore what faculty were doing on one campus (Southwest University) as it relates to the findings and recommendations of a recent campus climate study.

This study borrowed its central questions from Huberman and Miles (1984). In their research on the implantation of policy recommendations in the K–12 setting, they sought "to show just *what happened* in the course of these school improvement efforts, to explain *why* it happened, and to suggest the *implications* for changes . . . elsewhere" (Huberman & Miles, 1984, p. vi). Adapting this purpose to faculty-led change initiatives in a postsecondary setting, the analysis for the current study will address the following:

- *What* has happened at Southwest University to implement the recommendations set forth to improve the climate for women faculty and faculty of color by the Faculty Climate Project?
- If transformation has occurred subsequent to the Faculty Climate Project, *why* did it happen?
- *What* are the implications for change related to improving the campus climate for faculty at Southwest University?

Background

Southwest University is a large research-extensive institution and many of its programs are ranked among the top 10 universities in the nation. The university community employs over 14,000 individuals, including 1,540 instructional faculty (tenured and tenure-track instructional faculty, permanent lecturers, and other permanent faculty) and 841 nontenure-track faculty members. Of those 1,540 tenured and tenure-track faculty, 28.5% are women and 13% are people of color (4% are women of color; Office of Institutional Research, 2003–2004). The most recent data available for those faculty not on the tenure track show that 46.1% are women and 20.8% are people of color (7.9% are women of color) (Office of Institutional Research, 2002).

In addition to academic administrators (e.g., department chairs and deans) and staff, 2,384 employees occupy professional positions within the university. This particular category of professionals is incredibly diverse and includes, for example, some professionals whose work encompasses traditional faculty functions (e.g., research) and others whose primary role is managerial or administrative. Both the faculty phase and the staff phase of the Climate Project tried to address how these professionals experience campus climate, disaggregating them according to roles (i.e., faculty for Phase I and administration for Phase II). However, in both cases, the variation in that job category made it very difficult to have a complete picture of the experiences of those professionals and it is an area that warrants future investigation.

Faculty and University-Initiated Diversity Efforts

A number of organizations and committees at Southwest University are devoted to issues of diversity. One of the influences of the Faculty Climate Project has been an increase in the number of these organizations and how they intersect to achieve common goals of improving the recruitment, retention, promotion, work environment, and compensation of women faculty and faculty of color. Some of these groups, like the CSW, comprise faculty and administrators. Others, like those that are the focus of this investigation, were established and are led by faculty. It is the purpose of this study to better understand these faculty-led organizations and how they work to change the campus climate since the release of the Faculty Climate report.

The Organization for Faculty Women

The Organization for Faculty Women, founded by women faculty in 1982 as a membership organization aiming to support and advance women's position at Southwest University, has long been active in addressing such issues as salary equity, child and family care, and bringing women's concerns to the board of trustees. One of the founding members of OFW was the director of the Southwest Women's Studies program in 1982. She felt very strongly that the academic program needed to focus on becoming institutionalized academically in the university and that a complementary organization for faculty women could serve as a grassroots activist group to provide support for women faculty and to address issues germane to academic women on campus. Initially, the organization focused on addressing the vast gender-based salary inequities and gradually widened its scope to address issues related to benefits, campus climate, and improving leadership opportunities for academic women. Over time, the participation of faculty women has waxed and waned. Certain issues, like salary inequities, galvanized over 100 women to press the university administration to address this problem. It is possible that the tangible nature of that particular issue, coupled with the founding of a new organization (i.e., the OFW) not long after the height of second-wave feminism led to the vitality of the organization at that point in history. Moreover, later OFW issues, like campus climate, are more subjective and some benefit issues, like stopping the tenure clock, are not salient for all women.

As part of the OFW's activist strategies, it has worked closely with the university administration to address its concerns and foster change. The degree to which upper-level administrators have been open to working with OFW is also a catalyst for the peaks and valleys experienced by the women involved. Finally, the demands of faculty work have changed over time, with research productivity expectations increasing greatly, and faculty becoming increasingly more national and international in focus (rather than focused on the local community, as is the nature of activist work for the OFW; Fairweather, 1996). As a result, it is not surprising that the life cycle of OFW has also changed and will continue to change.

Faculty Climate Oversight Committee

The organization most closely resulting from phase 1 of the Faculty Climate Project at the university level is the Faculty Climate Oversight Committee. FCOC was established in 2002 by the president of Southwest University, and members were originally appointed by him, with strong recommendations from the original Faculty Climate Project chairs. More recently, new faculty members have been invited to join by existing FCOC members, based on their known skills in leadership and commitment to diversity issues. The list of FCOC members is forwarded to the president, who endorses each member's appointment at the beginning of the academic year.

Currently, the university-level FCOC has 24 regular and 5 ex officio members led by a chair and two cochairs. Members in FCOC are divided into three task forces, which parallel the areas of emphasis in the Faculty Climate Project itself: (a) Diverse, which focuses on issues of diversity in recruitment and retention; (b) Fair, which focuses on fair and equitable hiring, compensation, and workloads; and (c) Hospitable, which addresses issues of campus climate. Each of these FCOC task forces is cochaired by two or more faculty. The task force chairs and the overall FCOC chair and cochairs form the FCOC Executive Committee. This committee works to prioritize yearly initiatives and meets with the president and provost at least once per semester, both of whom have provided significant financial and political support for committee activities. While FCOC may be regarded as a faculty initiative, the goals are significantly enhanced by this support from upper administration.

College-Level FCOCs

Significant additions to the roster of organizations that have developed as a result of the Faculty Climate Project are the college-level FCOCs. The establishment of an oversight committee within each college was a priority of the universitywide FCOC, with strong support from the president's and provost's offices. The deans of each of the 15 colleges at Southwest were encouraged to develop these committees and about half of these colleges have formal committees. The establishment of college-level FCOCs was seen as the most effective means of carrying out Faculty Climate Project initiatives across a campus with highly disparate colleges.

Since the first establishment of college FCOCs during 2002–2003, there have been several means of integrating college and university FCOC activities. These include information-sharing meetings between the college FCOC chairs and the university FCOC and structured meetings focusing on best practices hosted by the university FCOC that deans and college FCOC chairs were invited to. Further integration of the two levels of FCOC has been enhanced by incorporating several college FCOC members into the universitywide FCOC task forces. Thus, the memberships of these faculty organizations overlap significantly—as do the memberships for all other organizations on campus devoted to diversity.

In sum, one of the major structural changes at Southwest University has been the expansion of the number of committees, task forces, and other faculty associations devoted to diversity since the Faculty Climate Project report was issued in 2001. Faculty leaders actively participate in these multiple organizations, which provide numerous opportunities to share goals and strategies. An important initiative within the universitywide FCOC was to promote the formation of college-level FCOCs that would be better placed to carry out initiatives particular to their academic settings, but with continued interaction with the universitywide FCOC. The intentional expansion of the universitywide FCOC to include members of the college-level FCOCs has added another layer of overlapping networks and provided opportunities for other faculty to learn how the university works. Some of the specific strategies are explored later in this study through focused analysis of two of the college FCOCs, as well as through the results of interviews with other campus organizations created before and after the Faculty Climate Project report was issued.

Methods
Sources of Data
As mentioned previously, faculty at Southwest University formed several task forces to address the recommendations from a campus-climate study. One

organization was not an outgrowth of the report; rather, the OFW was instrumental in the design and implementation of the study and continued to work on issues related to women faculty that emerged prior to, as a result of, and since the Faculty Climate Project report. Because of the strong ties of faculty-led organizations at Southwest University to the outcomes of the report, a purposive sample was drawn from those participating in efforts to implement recommendations related to the campus climate study.

The faculty members of the universitywide task force (FCOC) served as one of the focus groups interviewed for this study. In addition to this unique sample, two college FCOCs were identified as focus groups for this study. The setup process of each college-level FCOC differed considerably by college. For this study, two colleges (the college of science and the college of social science) that represent different histories of involvement in issues of campus climate and approaches to designating members of their FCOC were selected because of their maximum variation (Merriam, 1998). Finally, the members of the OFW made up another unique sample, because of the OFW's mission related to improving the campus climate for women faculty and its critical involvement in the original campus climate study. All participants in each of these groups were invited to participate, and those who were unable to attend the prescribed focus group meeting were invited to participate in individual interviews so that as many voices as possible could be captured related to these faculty-led change initiatives. Only the chair of the college of science FCOC chose to be interviewed individually, as he was unable to attend the focus group interview because of a scheduling conflict. Demographics of the 27 participants are broken down in Table 6.1.

Data Gathering and Analysis

A semistructured interview protocol (see appendix p. 159) was used for each focus group to loosely direct the conversation. The semistructured nature of the protocol allowed for the flow of the conversation to be guided; but the conversation was intentionally coconstructed by the interviewer and the participants in the focus groups. This process accommodated the emergence of unanticipated patterns and themes beyond the scope of the conceptual framework.

For this particularistic (Merriam, 1998), qualitative case study, transcripts and field notes from focus groups and documents were analyzed. Using a constant comparative approach (Strauss & Corbin, 1990), patterns and themes emerged from the data. These patterns and themes were then

TABLE 6.1
Participant Demographics

Focus/Discussion Group	Gender		Academic Rank						Race/Ethnicity					
	Female	Male	Prof	Assoc	Asst	Lecturer	Academic Professional	Other	White	African American/ Black	Native American	Asian American/ Pacific Islander	Hispanic	Other
FCOC Executive Committee	5	1	3	1	0	1	1	0	4	1	1	0	0	0
OFW	6	0	3	0	0	0	1	2	6	0	0	0	0	0
Social Science FCOC	4	3	1	3	2	0	1	0	5	1	0	0	1	0
Science FCOC	4	4	4	2	0	1	0	1	7	0	0	1	0	0
TOTALS	19	8	11	6	2	2	3	3	22	2	1	1	1	0

further analyzed to look for divergence and convergence. Trustworthiness of the findings was assured through triangulation of data sources (Patton, 1990) and saturation of categories (Lincoln & Guba, 1986). NVivo, a qualitative computer software package, was used to assist in managing the data throughout the analysis process.

Findings

FCOC

Participants in the FCOC described some characteristics that suggested they have been successful in their efforts to improve the campus climate at Southwest. First, those involved saw that organization itself has been sustained as one measure of success. Over the last 25 years at Southwest, at least three other climate studies had been completed without any significant changes attributable to the findings. In addition, there was no formal mechanism like the FCOC established to oversee initiatives related to study findings. The campus climate study in 2000–2001 was different in the eyes of those on the FCOC, and the fact that their oversight committee continued to solicit new members and to meet demonstrated a high degree of success. Second, one participant shared the following:

> if success is determined by consciousness raising, then I think that the administration or we can say that that has been achieved. The diversity, the fact that we are in this office, the diversity resource office, that there are staff members here, that there was the diversity day [are indicators of success]

Third, another concrete measure of success that members of the FCOC described was a workshop that the task force organized around the issue of cluster hiring, and another on subtle discrimination.

Despite these signs of success, the members of the FCOC were careful to temper their evaluation with some degree of hesitancy or marginality. For example, one participant said:

> Diversity is very visible and people say it all the time. It may be an empty phrase in a lot of their mouths, but it is said. It is recognized. People do pay obeisance to it and so on, which is better than nothing. It's not

everything. It's nowhere near everything, but it is something. I think that this committee had a lot to do with it.

In addition, participants in the FCOC focus group resoundingly expressed that the FCOC was a fairly invisible group on campus. This lack of visibility made it difficult to achieve any sort of success, institutionwide. While there was an articulated commitment to changing the campus climate among those on the FCOC, they felt hampered by the relative anonymity of the group itself. Several members of the FCOC also felt frustrated by the lack of leadership, particularly by the provost, on issues of diversity. This made their work difficult. Moreover, one member felt even members of the FCOC were beginning to lose energy and passion for the work at hand, as she said:

> I think that has been one of the underlying problems of implementing things because it has been not only the administration that doesn't see the value of implementing some of these things or understand the significance or the process of implementing these, but it is the people that are part of the oversight too.

The sense of frustration was also demonstrated by the members of the FCOC in how they understood power and change at the institution. While there was evidence, as cited above, that the FCOC could make some difference in terms of the climate at Southwest, several members of this focus group said that it was at the level of individual colleges or departments where change could really take place.

> And that's where a lot of the power is. It's in the colleges to be able to carry out oversight of their own FCOCs, actually to be able to establish them in the first place, to have oversight of those and then to develop what they take from their committee meetings and implement them from within the college.
>
> I have resigned from this committee. I am having some health issues that are stress related that are not all FCOC's fault. I had to make the choice of what am I going to cut out. And when I looked at what I was committed to in my department, in my college and in the University level, the place that I felt I was the most ineffective was at this level. So, if I had to cut something, I'm going to cut back to where I think I can actually be doing something that is going to be of value.

While some members of the FCOC saw the potential for change at more "local" levels (i.e., departments and colleges), all shared a dedication to improving the climate at Southwest, as is evident in their involvement in the university FCOC. In addition, many members participated in campus diversity efforts from multiple fronts, including college-level FCOCs and other universitywide diversity committees. The experiences of two college-level FCOCs are described below, and although the university FCOC members saw the potential for these organizations, the challenges faced by involved faculty on the university level were in many respects duplicated at the college level.

Colleges of Science and Social Science FCOCs

Faculty in the Colleges of Science and Social Science FCOCs felt that they had been able to make some impact on climates in their respective colleges. However, their sense of success was restrained and interestingly, without solicitation, participants in each group pointed to the other as having particularly effective characteristics.

> perhaps when there is a good connection between Social Science FCOCs and the dean's office. I get a sense that that works well through the College of Science. I get a sense that there is good communication there. Whatever that communication is happening, I think that is important. (Social Science FCOC)
>
> It's hard to keep optimism up. We've got so far to go, look at Social Science FCOC, who's on the march to achieving equity; here, we've just got the conversation going. (Science FCOC)

Reflecting on the effectiveness of another college FCOC suggests that while there are some things that have worked well for each group, there are also ways that these faculty-led initiatives could transform to be even more effective. Each has a lesson to learn from the other. However, each also has a very different set of circumstances, and those particularities seem to have an impact on the ways these organizations have operated.

First, the Science FCOC has a dean who has been financially supportive of the work of FCOC. He provided $25,000 to support the initiatives of the FCOC, matched by the office of the provost, and has recently begun to recognize that with some faculty within the college, especially women, problems and inequities continue to exist. Thus, with the active support of the dean, the chair of the Science FCOC purposefully invited a mix of people from every college department and managed the FCOC so that inactive members were removed from the committee.

> I didn't want the committee to consist entirely of people who department heads routinely nominate for this sort of work. Because I thought, if it was going to do anything, you also wanted a mix. You wanted also, some people who are not necessarily women. People who are not necessarily minorities, and I also wanted department heads to nominate people who were . . . you know carried some weight within their departments.

He also did not rely solely, or even primarily, on meetings to move the agenda of the FCOC forward. The group met about once each semester, but communicated electronically.

The outcome of the communications of the Science FCOC has been an initiative that was constructed on a data- and resource-driven scientific model. The primary focus for the FCOC has been directed on providing opportunities for individual departments to apply for funding to conduct research to address pipeline issues in a way that speaks to scientists. The Science FCOC chair explained:

> So, if you want scientists to actually do something different, you have to convince them that there really is something that needs to be done. And I thought that the way to do that is to have the science departments themselves do their own information gathering. . . . So, that was the underlying premise, was to get the departments to do some information gathering. To give them a certain amount of leeway as to exactly which area had to be related to diversity but within that framework, which area they chose to investigate. . . . Then we went to the provost and the dean, got some money, and started on this project.

Members of the Science FCOC supported these strategies, as they mirrored the priority to demonstrate evidence in their work as academics and to have autonomy in directing their own inquiry. They explained:

> We have a "research flair" here, it's what's going on, we're hands on.
>
> We're trying to create an environment of interest and knowledge, getting people to care. I don't think people are actively sexist or racist, but there's a culture of resignation that nothing will change. Our efforts are to

find sparks of interest; we're trying to make things not imposed from above. We did ask for money, too. It's a small amount of money, but there have been some successes.

The departments of physics, chemistry, mathematics, speech and hearing sciences, and geosciences have all received funding as a part of the Science FCOC grant effort, and some have finished reports based upon the research they have conducted in their departments. The chair of the Science FCOC hoped that in the fall all the reports will be completed and presented in a collegewide workshop. Already the fruits of one project from geosciences have had larger implications. Based upon the conceptual framework from Virginia Valian (1998), the data analysis from geosciences has resulted in a packet that the Science FCOC plans to distribute to hiring committees throughout the college. Yet, it is important to put these activities in the context described earlier. Although there have been tangible outcomes from the work of the Science FCOC, the women who participated in the science-based focus groups did not describe a markedly different climate as a result. Moreover, members of the Science FCOC also articulated some challenges and frustrations, and lack of success:

> The frustration is to see that people are interested in change, but now we are confronted by these [diversity] issues on a daily basis. I'm not necessarily feeling like we're having an effect.
>
> It is taking up time. I'm getting put on lots of committees because of my active involvement; I'm the "token white male."
>
> Will it be sustained? I'm running out of energy, and people are busy. Our best bet for sustaining is producing more active, interested, involved people. We need to get a number of people interested and educated.

Unlike the Science FCOC that took several semesters to coalesce, the Social Science FCOC was formed immediately following the release of the Faculty Climate Project report. Members of the committee saw costs as a result of being involved, as many activists in these sorts of faculty-led initiatives have already described. But they also shared that participation in the Social Science FCOC helped them feel part of something larger.

> You learn more than you would in your home unit: diversity, salary equity, lots of talk about salaries in the college.

So, one of the things that happens in this committee is that I learn about and know what is going on, be represented by all of my colleagues and we can exchange information that gives us all a better understanding of what Social Science is in the colleges.

This is a committee that does a lot of work. There is a cost because of the work. But the benefits are that "it is the right thing to do."

Within the organization of the Social Science FCOC, a college administrator attends and actively participates as an ad hoc member. This is different from the Science FCOC, as the dean and other administrative leaders at the college level are outside the actual FCOC process (other than to provide resources and verbal support). This sort of administrative participation has provided a sense of "realism" and advocacy to the university administration.

I think that having that ad hoc member of the committee certainly helps a lot. I feel that what we are doing here has made a difference and that there is a certain connection between the Provost's office and this has been a very important part of that.

[T]hat forces us to think within the box. It keeps us realistic, right, for better or for worse. But, we are not going to extend our energies, hopefully not expend our energies on things that are just pie in the sky.

Not only does the Social Science FCOC feel a connection to the provost, but one member of the current Social Science FCOC also served on the university FCOC. This relationship provided a mutually enhanced experience, and the member who served in a dual capacity felt that such a network was important.

In fact, administrative involvement on the Social Science FCOC was recognized as one of the reasons a primary initiative—how key personnel were allocated—was implemented.

And a department head here is also on this committee, or at least he was in the past, so that when they're at a head's and director's meeting and they say Social Science FCOC supports this, it was very hard with [one of our primary issues], for the heads and directors to argue with what Social Science FCOC had said. So, it was really effective, and without that, it would have been very difficult to get the heads to agree to a number of somewhat controversial aspects.

Whether administrative involvement was instrumental, the Social Science FCOC also highlighted other activities as indicative of some level of success, for example, creating a template for a consistent performance review process and initiating the Salary Equity Project.

However, members on the Social Science FCOC demonstrated some level of frustration in determining how effective and successful they had been:

> This is just a basic question about how do you measure something as elusive as the success rate on issues, particularly issues that are central to the Faculty Climate Project: hospitality and climate. How is that a measurable outcome?
>
> I think we are very much active in terms of trying to develop initiatives, but haven't gotten up to a point where we have a way of evaluating how successful we are. I don't know if that would help us in our objectives to have that kind of evaluation process. . . . but that is not what we explicitly have right now.
>
> I'm not sure we are successful. I think that we are successful in some ways. We are successful in the ways that are articulated in terms of being advisory, having a voice that is listened to within Social Science. We have been unsuccessful when we set out to try to make an initiative that requires funding and when we grow beyond Social Science's funding. That has been unsuccessful.

This ambivalence and uneven sense of success was a consistent feature in all the faculty-led initiatives under investigation in this research. Being critical of one's work and the work of others is part of faculty life, so perhaps it is not surprising that this theme continues to emerge. Yet, despite this degree of criticism and challenge, a modicum of influence and an unmitigated commitment toward diversity for those involved can be teased out.

OFW

Like the FCOC, the OFW identified specific policies and practices that these faculty felt contributed to an improved campus climate for women and other underrepresented populations. Specifically, women in the OFW focus group described how important it was for the campus to have policies so that the tenure clock can be stopped twice and/or alternative work duties can be negotiated for childbirth or adoption. They also identified the comprehensive salary study that OFW helped to conduct in the early 1980s that resulted in significant salary adjustments based on gender gaps in pay. In all these cases, it was because of the persistence of women involved in OFW that the policies and practices were ultimately implemented, earning this organization specific measures of success and wide-ranging support from women faculty.

Less tangible measures of success were also identified. In fact, one woman explained that policy change might be less important than the following, with regard to the legacy of success of the OFW:

> [F]or those of us that are in parts of campus where you rarely see other women . . . I walked into [the] fall OFW reception probably in '89, I would guess, and there were probably 75 women in the house. And I came home and said to my husband, "Oh my god, there are women on this campus!" I had been here seven years and I had seen one. And here were 75 all in one room. So, it was finding out that there was a lifeboat out there that has got people in it. But whether there were ever issues addressed, to some extent, did not matter.

Moreover, the longevity of the organization, which has been on campus for 23 years, reminds administrators on campus and the campus community more broadly, that the organization still has work to do and is not going away quietly. One way these women faculty do this is by meeting regularly with the president, provost, and board of regents to identify issues salient to women faculty on campus and to suggest potential solutions to improve the climate. While these meetings are often considered congenial opportunities to talk with upper-level administrators, one woman shared a different perspective:

> There is some fear factor, perhaps among the Provost and President, associated with when OFW comes to town, I think. . . . which is a good thing.

In addition to the tangible measures of success, members of the OFW discussed the nature of the organization, bringing together women from disciplines throughout the university. This cross- and interdisciplinary organization had the potential to find common ground among faculty. While some common ground has been found, as described in the successes above, there is still a sense that these women faculty operate at cross-purposes. For example, one OFW member described:

I was hoping that in OFW, we can have more of a discussion that is across the disciplines, because I find that very much that there are unique cultures in each college with a completely different idea of the universe. . . . We are not helping with the dialogue with how to better do what we are supposed to be doing. We are not all agreeing with what we are supposed to be doing.

Further, the complexity of human relationships and the life course of an organization like OFW not only influenced the nature of success for this organization, but also the nature of change. The women in OFW understand that change is slow, and perhaps it is this understanding that has led to the sustainability (albeit with differing levels of momentum) over time. In fact, one woman compared change in the academy to change in the Catholic Church—exceedingly slow. She continued the parallels between the church and the university as she shared the following:

I see that universities have deep monastic roots. You walk into a lecture hall and it's set up like a church. We've got an altar in front. We have our T.A. acolytes aside. Nobody has given me a bell yet to ring, but . . . you know, we have our robes and gowns and things that we wear at certain times. I just think that whole "High Church" culture is so deeply ingrained. You know, you take the vow of poverty . . . and my husband thinks chastity as well. You get hired here and there is the same marginalization of women in the academy that there is in the Church.

The women in the OFW experienced frustrations, that many of the issues that were identified as needing to be addressed at the time of the interview were the same issues the OFW identified when data were collected for the Faculty Climate Project and when the OFW was founded in 1982. These challenges shaped the perspectives of the women in the OFW about what success should truly mean. What emerged for women involved in this faculty-led change initiative was that the very definition of success that permeates the discourse at the university was highly problematic. The following passage from one of the OFW participants got to the heart of the matter:

Whose standards are we using? Who gets to define those standards? Going back to your question on how successful we have been in this initiative, I don't see any discussion of the definitions having changed. I really don't. I do not see a real frank discussion about it.

The definition of success is based exclusively on quantitative measures that are differentially valued based upon resources and research. Less tangible, qualitative measures, like diversity or respect, do not get rewarded or are deemed successful in the institution's discourse. Another participant illustrated this perspective in the following example:

> You wouldn't go to the State Legislature and say: "I need a 10 million dollar salary package, because there's just not enough respect at Southwest!" You go because Georgia Tech hired four chemists. You say, "Boy, if you'd just given me a 40 million dollar building, I would have had four more chemists.". . . . But, fundamentally, it comes down to respect: who gives respect, who gets respect. More often than not, we are losing people because of a respect issue.

In the end, where the OFW has experienced the most frustration and challenge was in trying to broaden and legitimate a definition of success that includes diversity, respect, and the voices of women and other underrepresented groups.

Discussion

What Happened?

First, it is important to understand who participated in these faculty-led change initiatives at Southwest University in order to capture the complexities of what happened. Demographic data of those participating in focus groups for this study show that most of the faculty who were involved in the change initiatives were faculty with tenure. In addition, most of the change agents participating were women and most were white. The percentage of people of color involved in these particular initiatives was slightly below the institutional demographics.

When looking at the success of these faculty-led change initiatives related to implementing the recommendations of a campus climate study, the results were mixed. The findings were uneven in every one of the organizations explored for this study. For the faculty on the university and college-level FCOCs, they pointed to instances of success and also of failure, but in most cases, these measures were quantifiable. Particularly in the College of Science, efforts were gauged on a scientific and positivistic model. The nature of the field influenced what strategies were used and how they were measured. Even with an interdisciplinary initiative like the OFW, faculty mentioned the influences of discipline and how they can shape the direction the organization takes. However, the women in the OFW also described a broader definition of success that can rely on the quantifiable results but also include qualitative measures, like climate, respect, and diversity.

Overall, college-level initiatives, analyzed through focus group interviews with the Colleges of Science and Social Science FCOCs, suggested that faculty in some colleges have worked very hard to create processes and recommendations, based upon a model that reinforces the very nature of faculty work. This professionalized activism (Hart, in 2005) demonstrated that activities like funding, collecting, and analyzing college-specific data (i.e., research); attending and presenting professional development sessions and workshops on issues of diversity (i.e., teaching); and meeting as a committee to consider the climate in each college (i.e., service) were very much a part of the way some faculty engaged in change initiatives related to the campus climate study.

Like the faculty involved in the college-level initiatives, the faculty participating in the university FCOC and OFW focus groups expressed a commitment to the original campus climate study and to improving the climate, although findings suggested the campus was not as fair, hospitable, and diverse as they hoped. The faculty involved in the university FCOC and OFW described strategies and activities in line with professionalized activism, similar to the initiatives described by the college-level FCOCs. Moreover, these faculty identified specific policies and practices that emerged from their professionalized activism that resulted in some measure of success in terms of campus climate. However, stories from the women in the OFW outlined the inadequacy of a "traditional" interpretation of success for the study, suggesting that it is incomplete. It failed to recognize that standards of success, as hooks (1993) argued, are different for those who are underrepresented and oppressed in the academy.

How Faculty Worked with Administration

How faculty worked with administrators varied, based upon the particular organization. The organizations that also included representation of administrators (i.e., dean's office representation in the College of Social Science FCOC and department chair representation in the College of Science

FCOC) saw that collaborating and partnering with administrative leadership were critical to the success of their diversity efforts. While some faculty participating in the university FCOC and in the College of Science FCOC were more cynical and less apt to embrace alliances with the administration, the groups themselves were based upon a certain degree of administrative appointment, and in the case of the College of Science FCOC, its primary strategies were reliant on the goodwill and resources of the dean and provost to fund them. This connection and the involvement of administrators in these groups meant that some of the faculty reluctance and caution was tempered with a perceived need to work directly with the administration to achieve success. This strategy has been referred to as creating prestige networks (fostering relationships with those in traditional university leadership roles in order to advance the organization's agenda; Hart, 2003). The author originally coined this term to describe the nature of the relationships that the OFW fostered as part of its activist agenda. Like professionalized activism, OFW continues to use a certain degree of prestige networking. However, the women faculty involved in the organization at the time the data for this study were collected articulated a shifting strategy. These women saw their roles now as more adversarial to the administration and as serving as monitors to ensure that the administration was aware of the diversity issues that remain unresolved, even though they continue to meet with and work with the university administration in order to advance their activist agenda.

Why Did It Happen?

The demographic breakdown of participation among change agents was not surprising. One would expect that those who appeared to have more legitimate power (i.e., faculty with tenure and white faculty) would serve in leadership roles and would seek to protect those who are most vulnerable. In fact, at a research university like Southwest University, it is the socialized norm to protect the research time of junior faculty by limiting or eliminating their service activities, despite the potential benefits of service for creating a sense of belonging and self-worth (Boice, 2000) and for facilitating helpful networking and mentoring. Thus, this important work is relinquished to their more senior colleagues. In addition, serving on committees dedicated to activism and change rarely "count" in the promotion, tenure, and review processes. Further, working toward institutional transformation is a risky undertaking. Faculty involved in such work are often considered "agitators" and "troublemakers" (Theodore, 1986), so faculty who do not have the security of tenure (including those not on the tenure track) might be less likely to engage in change initiatives. Yet, it is also important to note that while the change initiatives are intended to address climate in a broad sense, faculty issues are the most salient for these activists. Additionally, faculty issues related to being on the tenure track are particularly pronounced, and the distinct issues faced by over 40% of the faculty who do not have a tenured or tenure-track appointment are unnoticeable.

However, the gender breakdown and the fact that so many of those involved in change efforts were faculty of color paint a different picture.[2] In a documented climate (as evidenced in the climate study that precipitated the change initiatives under investigation) where women and faculty of color experience inequities, including subtle and less-subtle forms of harassment, women and some faculty of color were among the most active in trying to improve the overall experience for themselves and their colleagues. The campus climate study at Southwest University clearly described an experience where women and faculty of color felt overburdened by and unrewarded and unappreciated for their service; yet, evidence from the current study reinforced that it was these same faculty (particularly women) who were championing the service work involved in these change initiatives. This finding clearly supports work done by Bird, Litt, and Wang (2004); Baez (2000); and Turner and Thompson (1993), which suggested that women and faculty of color were often drawn to academic "institutional housekeeping" (Bird et al., 2004, p. 194), a purposeful term intended to reclaim the significance of housekeeping as legitimate and meaningful.

For those faculty involved in universitywide change efforts (e.g., FCOC and OFW) and in the Science and Social Science FCOCs, they overwhelmingly articulated an almost visceral need to work toward improving the campus climate. This agenda was so important to these faculty that they chose to participate despite the lack of reward related to their faculty work. Many faculty who participated in each focus group expressed frustration because of a perceived lack of institutional commitment on the part of institutional leaders (particularly the provost) in such change efforts. Given that the faculty participating in this study described using a strategy of prestige networking (Hart, 2003) by working with the university president and provost (or in the case of the college-level FCOCs, the college dean) to initiate transformation, institutional leadership that appeared disengaged, disinterested, or hostile to change efforts ultimately hindered any positive climate change.

The stories told in this study were often discouraging. There was an overall impression among the faculty that while there were moments where aspects of campus climate had the potential to improve and sustain themselves, there were as many moments (if not more) where efforts were stagnated and even regressed. The underlying lesson learned was that change is slow. The women faculty in the OFW understood this, as demonstrated by the longevity of the organization and the tenacity of the faculty involved in it. They also articulated new ways to construct their activism. Specifically, they identified "guerrilla warfare" as one strategy they use to work for change. This means that they feel that working against the power structure, rather than with it, is sometimes necessary to build a more hospitable and equitable environment. Unlike the tactics described in a previous study of the OFW (Hart, 2005), these women began to see themselves as activist professionals (Hart), maintaining their professional academic role as faculty women, but foregrounding their activism as a way to keep the administration in check. Time involved in change initiatives and an organizational history may explain why the OFW was frustrated, but did not see giving up or getting out of activist work as an option, whereas faculty in the other focus groups were more willing to consider abandoning the initiatives.

Implications

The findings from this study have several implications. First, the nature of faculty-led initiatives is complex. Who participates and how they participate vary widely. Gender, race, ethnicity, discipline, academic rank, and ideas of success further complicate what faculty-led initiatives look like at Southwest University. For instance, in Chronister, Gansneder, Harper, and Baldwin, "[b]etween 1976 and 1993, the number of non-tenure track full-time faculty increased by 142% for women and 54% for men" (as cited in Perna, 2001, p. 585). This means as workers in a broad category, the numbers of nontenure-track faculty continue to grow. Given the clustering of women in these positions nationally and the degree to which they have become a significant portion of the instructional workforce in academe (which undoubtedly has an influence on the numbers of faculty of color as well), it is critical that faculty-led change initiatives are considering these faculty as they work to transform institutions. Yet, studies like this one indicate that this growing cadre of faculty is often forgotten or ignored in the important work faculty change agents are engaging in. Further, while there was some evidence of the need to explore diversity beyond gender and race/ethnicity, other aspects like sexual orientation, age, religion, social class, and the intersectionality of diversity issues also remain marginal.

Second, some faculty in this study have felt an overwhelming sense of discouragement and frustration. However, these faculty were extremely committed to improving campus climate and creating an environment at Southwest University that is more diverse, hospitable, and fair. These faculty were interested in social justice, the value diversity adds to education, and in the institution itself. The faculty "brain drain" has been an issue of fundamental concern at this campus, and issues of faculty retention are significant nationwide. Institutional leaders can and should capitalize on loyal and dedicated faculty. Faculty involved in change initiatives related to campus climate were trying to reduce faculty attrition directly and indirectly—and such work should be legitimately rewarded. Further, the faculty involved already have strong institutional loyalty, and the university should think very seriously about how leaders can work with faculty activists to maintain that loyalty. Faculty change agents who have been involved in climate work for years will become disenfranchised if institutions don't respond to the dedication and service they provide. This ultimately means that institutional housekeeping must be institutionalized and valorized, not marginalized. Faculty and university leaders must reclaim service as a vital part of institutional transformation and academic excellence (Bennett, 1998; Bird et al., 2004).

Further, if domination and patriarchy are part of the organization and operation of the academy (hooks, 1993), then in order to witness success, a new definition must be created, one that includes diversity and respect and is not measured solely according to a model supposedly based on a meritocracy. Working with institutional leaders, through prestige networking and using professionalized activist strategies may result in an improved campus climate for diversity; however, faculty activists must consider whether the strategies they use serve to replicate the patriarchy and an existing model of success or whether they must be expanded (this is to suggest that it does not have to be an either/or phenomenon, but can be a both/and) to craft a new and vibrant model of success that dismantles hierarchy and domination.

Conclusion

In a time in academe when many campuses are assessing the climate for underrepresented groups of faculty and are making specific recommendations
about what campuses need to do to enhance the climate to ensure academic
excellence (National Academy of Sciences, 2004), it is critical that these reports do not sit on a shelf and collect dust. Rather, it is imperative that campuses are taking these reports, as evidenced by some events at MIT (Koerner,
1999) and at Southwest University, and work to level the academic playing
field. This case study provided evidence of how faculty on one campus has
tried to work toward change, specifically toward creating a more diverse, hospitable, and fair campus climate. The results are mixed, but in all cases, there
is much to be learned from these events. Faculty on other campuses may be
able to adapt the successes and avoid the mistakes described in this study to
foster a climate at their college or university that will prevent further marginalization of underrepresented groups in academe.

References

Baez, B. (2000). Race-related service and faculty of color: Conceptualizing critical
agency in academe. *Higher Education, 39,* 363–391.
Bennett, J. B. (1998). *Collegial professionalism: The academy, individualism, and the
common good.* Phoenix, AZ: Oryx Press/American Council on Higher Education.
Bird, S., Litt, J., & Wang, Y. (2004). Creating status of women reports: Institutional
housekeeping as "women's work." *NWSA Journal, 16*(1), 194–206.
Boice, R. (2000). *Advice for new faculty members: Nihil nimus.* Boston: Allyn &
Bacon.
Cress, C. (2001). *The faculty climate project: Report in detail.* Southwest University,
Office of the President.
Cress, C., Dinnerstein, M., Miller, N. J., & Hart, J. (2001). *The faculty climate proj-
ect: Summary report.* Southwest University, Office of the President.
Fairweather, J. (1996). *Faculty work and public trust: Restoring the value of teaching
and public service in American academic life.* Boston: Allyn & Bacon.
Hart, J. (2003, November). *Creating networks as an activist strategy: Differing approaches among academic feminist organizations.* Paper presented at the Association for the Study of Higher Education Annual Conference, Portland, OR.
Hart, J. (2005, Summer). Activism among feminist academics: Professionalized activism and activist professionals. *Advancing Women in Leadership.* Retrieved June
7, 2005, from http://www.advancingwomen.com/awl/social_justice1/Hart.html
hooks, b. (1993). Keeping close to home: Class and education. In M. M. Tokarczyk &

E. A. Fay (Eds.), *Working-class women in the academy: Laborers in the knowledge factory.* Amherst: University of Massachusetts Press.

Huberman, A. M., & Miles, M. B. (1984). *Innovation up close.* New York: Plenum.

Johnsrud, L. K., Perreira, D. C., Miller, U. K., Inoshita, L. T., & Hart, J. L. (2002). *The staff climate project phase II: Classified staff and appointed personnel. Summary report: Vol 1. Appendices: Vol. 2.* Southwest University: Office of the President.

Koerner, B. I. (1999, April 5). The boys' club persists: MIT acknowledges it has a female problem: Discrimination. *U.S. News & World Report, 126*(13), 56.

Lincoln, Y., & Guba, E. (1986). *Naturalistic inquiry.* Newbury Park, CA: Sage.

Massachusetts Institute of Technology. (1999). *A study on the status of women faculty in science at MIT.* Retrieved January 27, 2000, from http://web.mit.edu/fnl/women/women.html

Merriam, S. B. (1998). *Qualitative research and case study application in education.* San Francisco: Jossey-Bass.

National Academy of Sciences. (2004). *Gender faculty studies at Research 1 institutions.* Retrieved July 30, 2004, from http://www7.nationalacademies.org/cwse/gender_faculty_links.html

Office of Institutional Research. (2002). *Integrated Postsecondary Education Data System: Fall staff survey.*

Office of Institutional Research. (2003–2004). *Southwest University fact book.*

Patton, M. Q. (1990). *Qualitative evaluation and research methods.* Newbury Park, CA: Sage.

Perna, L. W. (2001). The relationship between faculty responsibilities and employment status among college and university faculty. *Journal of Higher Education, 72*(5), 584–611.

Strauss, A., & Corbin, J. (1990). *Basics of qualitative research: Grounded theory procedures and techniques.* Newbury Park, CA: Sage.

Theodore, A. (1986). *The campus troublemakers: Academic women in protest.* Houston, TX: Cap and Gown Press.

Turner, C. S. V., & Thompson, R. J. (1993). Socializing women doctoral students: Minority and majority experiences. *Review of Higher Education, 16*(3), 355–370.

Valian, V. (1998). *Why so slow? The advancement of women.* Cambridge, MA: MIT Press.

Notes

1. Southwest University is a pseudonym used to further ensure the confidentiality of those who participated in this study. All subsequent references related to this university are masked.

2. It should be reinforced that the College of Science FCOC was intentional in establishing its committee to create an organization that relied less on those who are often overburdened by service. But when looking at these organizations in the aggregate, women in particular were overrepresented as activists.

7

CONCLUSION

Ann E. Austin

E ach of the chapters in this book addresses an important aspect of academic work and workplaces. As a group, they offer a set of important themes for institutional leaders and faculty members to consider. Here, I highlight several of the issues brought forth in these chapters.

Strength and Impact of the Maternal Wall

A major work/family issue in academe pertains to the experiences of women faculty who bear and raise children. Several of the chapters address this issue and suggest that the "maternal wall" is still quite strong, creating a barrier that sometimes impedes the advancement of faculty members who are mothers. Mason, Goulden, and Wolfinger in their chapter, "Babies Matter: Pushing the Gender Equity Revolution Forward," provide data showing that, despite the increasing number of women working in academe, barriers associated with having babies remain strong. Women still constitute only 26% of the faculty, and women scholars who have early babies, which they define as within the first five years of receiving a Ph.D., are more likely to hold nontenure-track positions. Furthermore, married men with children under six are 50% more likely than married women with children under six to take a tenure-stream position within the first year after the Ph.D. Overall, getting married and having babies decreases the chance that a female scholar will enter the tenure track.

Other aspects of the maternal wall are explored in the Wolf-Wendell and Ward chapter, "Faculty Work and Family Life: Policy Perspectives from

Different Institutional Roles." Their research on the experiences of junior faculty who are mothers and their perceptions of the policy context and environment within higher education institutions for faculty with children reveal disturbing stereotypes. Women reported being hesitant about taking available leaves for childbirth because of concerns about the reactions of their colleagues. Their respondents also offered examples of stressful and embarrassing moments they endured because colleagues were unaccustomed to dealing with the physical needs of new mothers (such as the need to find a quiet, private place for breast pumping). Together these chapters provided a range of evidence about the continuing existence of how the "maternal wall" creates challenges for women scholars seeking to secure positions, advance once they have positions, and manage their maternal duties along with their professional responsibilities.

Influence of the Career on the Family

Another theme within the chapters is that, for faculty members, family not only affects career, but career experiences affect family. Mason, Goulden, and Wolfinger report that 12 years out from the Ph.D. a minority of ladder-rank women are married and have children. The data from their research indicate that women faculty are more likely than male colleagues to delay childbirth into their late 30s. Furthermore, women faculty in their study from the University of California between ages 40 and 60 were twice as likely as men to have fewer children than they wanted. Their conclusion is that the academic structures and practices inhibit family formation for women faculty. A skeptic might argue that any demanding career—faculty work, law, medicine, for example—may require personal sacrifices and that the choice resides with the individual to decide whether to make the necessary sacrifices. Few would probably disagree with that assertion. The concern raised by the Mason, Goulden, and Wolfinger work is that women are finding it necessary to make more personal sacrifices than their male colleagues. The level of sacrifice does not hold constant for all members of the academy but rather significantly disadvantages one major group. Returning to the arguments offered earlier in this chapter, I am concerned that, if the American academy aspires to having a diverse group of faculty members, including both significant numbers of women as well as men, then institutional policies must be adjusted to enable women to pursue academic careers without experiencing disproportionate sacrifices to their personal lives. Otherwise, some talented women will not choose this career route.

Creamer's chapter on the early-career experiences of co-working academic couples—dual-career couples who collaborate together—adds another perspective on how work structures and polices affect family and personal relationships. In order to be sure each member of the couple is taken seriously, couples sometimes conceal their working relationship until after tenure is granted. For example, they may not list both individuals as co-authors until posttenure. Institutional policies that do not value or support collaborative work may lead to such couples choosing to relocate after the tenure decision in order to find more "couple-friendly" institutional environments. Thus, the impact of institutional reward structures that emphasize what Creamer calls "individualistic values" may result in geographic disruption for a family as well as the loss of academic talent for a university or college.

Strategies Faculty Use to Juggle Professional and Personal Responsibilities

Several of the chapters shed light on how faculty members—women as well as men—manage their academic work and their personal responsibilities. Based on an intensive qualitative study of faculty time, Colbeck's chapter explores balance, integration, flexibility, and permeability between work and personal roles. Her research shows that faculty members do not all prefer or choose the same strategies. Some prefer to find opportunities to integrate their work and personal roles by sometimes addressing simultaneously the demands of both worlds. For example, some faculty may work at home writing a paper while also supervising children and stopping occasionally to advise about homework and prepare meals. Others prefer to balance but separate their attention to various demands. Colbeck also found that the female faculty she studied protected their time at work (avoiding interruptions for personal matters) more than male faculty did. She also learned that some faculty realize more than their colleagues that they have options to make choices about how they allocate their time and the strategies they use for managing their work and personal responsibilities.

Making choices about how to organize one's work and, more broadly, one's life, continues throughout the career. Even though early-career faculty may have worked through, over time, the ways they will organize their responsibilities, they usually must revisit and modify their choices once tenure is achieved. Neumann, Terosky, and Schell suggest that the work of developing strategies is part of the life course for everyone, but that individual faculty members vary in the prominence they give to their scholarly agendas, the ways they envision and achieve a sense of balance in their lives, and the coping strategies they enlist to deal with frustrations.

As mentioned, Creamer studied couples who engage in work collaboratively. Like Colbeck, she found that they employed a range of strategies to accommodate their personal and professional lives. Strategies included choosing collaborative work as an explicit means to enable them to juggle personal and professional interests—that is, collaboration as a strategy to accomplish each scholar's career goals while also enhancing their personal lives. Other strategies were to take turns as first author, to establish independent research identities in addition to their collaborative work, and to "dazzle" colleagues with the number of their publications.

Wolf-Wendel and Ward's chapter on institutional policies at various institutional types pertaining to faculty with children also shows that individuals develop a range of strategies to handle child-related responsibilities while they fulfill work obligations. Often, however, the strategies available to women are at some risk to themselves. For example, women in the study reported returning to work quickly after childbirth, forgoing appropriate personal care. Others arranged leaves on their own, finding colleagues to cover their classes when they delivered babies. While the strategy ensured that the female faculty member knew professional responsibilities were covered while she was out, she often had no institutional help to find course coverage. Additionally, these young faculty members, often new to the institution and untenured, feel they may be jeopardizing the goodwill of their colleagues in ways that will jeopardize their long-term career success. Hart's detailing of the faculty pathways and negotiations at one university provides a backdrop for developing more proactive strategies.

These chapters suggest that many work/family issues are appropriately handled through the plans and according to the preferences of the individual faculty member, and that academic work provides a fair amount of flexibility that helps faculty members manage their multiple responsibilities. Yet these studies also suggest that faculty members typically solve the challenge of managing personal and professional responsibilities on their own, with only minimal institutional help. And sometimes the strategies women find necessary tax their well-being. Some of the dilemmas faculty face with regard to the management of work and personal responsibilities could be aided by appropriate institutional policies.

Institutional Policies Pertaining to Work and Personal Responsibilities

Ideally, universities and colleges have developed and implemented institutional policies to address some of the challenges faculty face in managing personal and professional responsibilities. But a number of institutions, as suggested by Wolf-Wendel and Ward's study, do not yet have such policies in place. These authors argue that the lack of policies and reasonable practices concerning childbirth and parental responsibilities inhibits the ability of faculty members to do good work. For example, without convenient locations for breast-feeding, faculty who are new mothers are left to deal with uncomfortable, embarrassing, or inconvenient situations as they try to fulfill this parental responsibility—and these avoidable situations detract from their efforts to focus while at work on professional responsibilities.

Some institutions, however, are setting excellent examples in offering and encouraging their faculty to use policies pertaining to work and personal responsibilities. For example, some institutions offer "active service/modified duties" for faculty members with particular personal responsibilities, as well as tenure-clock extension or stoppage options for faculty with new children or other personal circumstances. Even when policies to address personal and professional responsibilities are in place, however, faculty members often do not use them. As these chapters point out, the reasons vary. Faculty members may not be aware of policies relevant to their situations, or they may fear colleagues who are inconvenienced or external reviewers of their tenure and promotion files who will not look favorably on leaves associated with personal matters. "Bias avoidance" (Drago & Williams, 2000), the effort of an employee to try to conform to ideal norms of what it means to be a productive, successful, and good worker, is another reason faculty members hesitate to use available work/family policies.

As discussed in the previous paragraphs, faculty members find ways to cope. However, institutions could support more fully their faculty members who have personal responsibilities by reviewing and publicizing the available policies and options. Such information is relevant to many faculty members—

men and women, faculty in different types of appointments, and faculty at different career stages. Institutional attention to providing, publicizing, and encouraging the use of policies that help faculty deal with professional and personal responsibilities will both enhance the quality of the environment, making it more attractive to potential faculty members, and help individual scholars fulfill professional and personal duties.

Issues Vary by Institutional Type

The chapters in this monograph offer research based on a variety of institutional types, including research universities, liberal arts colleges, comprehensive institutions, and community colleges. The data and findings suggest that faculty members' issues concerning the relationship of work and personal responsibilities may vary somewhat across institutional types. Faculty members at a research university may have some flexibility about the number of courses they are expected to teach in a given semester and the time they spend on campus, which may help during periods when home responsibilities increase. As Wolf-Wendel and Ward indicate, however, their counterparts at a community college may face heavy teaching loads every semester as well as expectations to hold required office hours. The research university professor, however, may feel hesitant about taking a leave that will affect the professor's research productivity or trajectory, knowing that research productivity is a key component of tenure considerations.

Such findings about the particular issues facing faculty at different institutional types suggest that policies will need to be considered within the context of institutional cultures. Traditions, expectations, and reward structures will vary across institutional types, and even within similar institutions, individual cultures are different. Institutional policies to enhance the quality of the academic workplace should take into account the particularities of the relevant context.

Implications for Action

As the demographic profile of the faculty body becomes more diverse, faculty members are likely to vary in the circumstances of their lives. Although all faculty members can be expected to bring expertise, creativity, and commitment to the hard work required to succeed as a scholar, they have different needs and challenges as they handle their work and personal responsibilities. Some faculty members continue to fit the traditional profile of a full-time professor (typically male) with a spouse working in the home to handle personal responsibilities. Other faculty members may be young female scholars balancing work duties along with preparation for the imminent birth of a child, single parents (men or women) juggling work and family, members of dual-career couples each trying to engage in demanding work, or individuals in a number of other circumstances. Recognition that the American academy needs the talents of an array of faculty members, including those who are committed to including and fulfilling personal and professional responsibilities in their lives, is a first step in creating more supportive and productive academic work environments. With this recognition, institutional leaders and faculty members can work together to examine the nature of the academic workplace and ensure that appropriate policies and practices are in place. Here I suggest some strategies for action for institutional leaders and faculty members. I also include a note specifically for faculty members involved in preparing doctoral students to serve as the next generation of faculty.

Strategies for Institutional Leaders

Those serving in institutional leadership roles as administrators or faculty members can begin by considering how the relationship of professional and personal dimensions of faculty lives are framed and discussed. Is the issue presented as an opportunity to ensure the excellence of the institution and the work that faculty members do? For example, leaders can explain that the university or college values a diverse faculty, recognizes that individual faculty members face different personal circumstances, and is committed to policies that help faculty members manage professional and personal responsibilities so they can do excellent scholarly work.

Institutional leaders also should assess the needs of the faculty, the relevant policies that are in place, and those policies that should be developed. The research reported in this monograph suggests that institutions are most effective in addressing faculty work/life issues when they ensure that a package of policies is available. No single policy or strategy can address the variety of issues confronting faculty members managing professional and personal responsibilities. As discussed in the Mason, Goulden, and Wolfinger chapter, institutions such as the University of California at Berkeley have developed policies, among others, pertaining to maternity and parental leave, child care, relocation, and temporary part-time assignments for tenure-stream faculty.

Even when policies are in place, however, such as for parental leave or for temporary modified duties, faculty members often do not use them. They may be unaware of the options, fearful that they will jeopardize their professional futures, or concerned about inconveniencing their colleagues. Leaders need to ensure not only that policies are in place, but also that the use of the policies is considered normal and routine. For example, some department chairs automatically work with pregnant faculty to arrange leave, which frees an individual faculty member from the need to raise the issue at all. With greater routine associated with the use of policies, stigma, fear, and reluctance surrounding their use will diminish.

As policies are reviewed, developed, and implemented, leaders should take special note of the language used in documents and conversation. For example, discussing maternity as a "problem" to be addressed through sick leave is different from discussing it as a normal circumstance to be handled through routine policies. Discussing a faculty applicant in a dual-career situation as a "two-body problem" suggests deviance or abnormality; even a slight change in language to "two-body situation" or "two-body opportunity" conveys a different and more positive message.

Department chairs hold critical roles in ensuring that faculty are aware of policies and in encouraging them to use available options. Chairs can shape the language used within a department and take the initiative to provide information and options relevant to the situation of each faculty member. They can be alert to seemingly small issues such as the scheduling of meetings or classes that, with attention, can be handled in ways that help faculty members manage multiple responsibilities (as mentioned in the monograph, for example, late-afternoon meetings that extend past 5 p.m. may interfere with the responsibility of some faculty members to pick up children at day care by a certain time). Many department chairs, while eager to support the excellence of their faculty members, may have thought little about the different circumstances of their faculty in regard to work/family balance. Chairs can benefit from professional development opportunities that highlight institutional policies concerning faculty appointments and work/life and that offer guidance to chairs about how to discuss these matters with their faculty.

In addition to ensuring that appropriate policies are available and widely known, provosts and deans can set up systems for monitoring the use and impact of policies related to faculty work issues. Regularly collecting institutional data enables leaders to determine how and under what circumstances policies are used, whether faculty in some parts of the institution are not using the options available, and how policies could be made more effective and beneficial for the institution as a whole and for faculty members individually. Additionally, leaders can work with faculty members to develop research agendas pertaining to faculty life and the quality of the academic workplace. Pursuing a research agenda on these issues provides data for institutional decision making and symbolically indicates that senior institutional leaders consider issues concerning the relationship between professional and personal responsibilities to be of importance to the quality and excellence of the institution. As institutions experiment with various policies intended to address issues concerning faculty roles and responsibilities, data on successes and problems also should be shared explicitly so other universities and colleges can benefit and learn.

Strategies for Faculty Members

Presidents, provosts, deans, and department chairs cannot alone be responsible for the quality of the academic workplace. Individual faculty members must also take interest in the institutional culture as it relates to faculty life. The chapter authored by Wolf-Wendel and Ward illustrates poignantly how colleague attitudes and lack of knowledge and sensitivity can exacerbate the challenges for faculty who are parents. Colleagues who themselves have traditional family and career patterns may need to broaden their awareness of the circumstances of others. All faculty members should be informed about institutional policies concerning faculty work. Departmental committees on faculty affairs could disseminate regularly relevant policy information to ensure wide knowledge and the development of a departmental culture that recognizes and supports the various circumstances of a diverse faculty.

Strategies for Preparing the Next Generation of Faculty

Doctoral students who are considering faculty roles sometimes express concern about the pace of activity in the lives of the faculty members they know, and wonder whether they want to pursue such careers. Some muse explicitly over the challenges of balancing work with family and personal commitments (Austin, 2002; Nyquist et al., 1999; Rice, Sorcinelli, & Austin, 2000).

Today's doctoral students need to see the various kinds of lives that faculty members live. They also need to know that, as faculty members, they can make choices about how to organize their professional and personal lives; that balance, flexibility, and integration of professional and personal responsibilities are handled in various ways; and that successful faculty members do not all follow the same patterns in their choices. Department chairs, graduate directors, and advisors should arrange for formal information sessions and informal conversations designed to help prospective faculty prepare for making their own choices about career and personal life. Such sessions could address the various institutional types in which they might work (which offer different settings for managing professional and personal balance), the choices they should consider as they plan their careers, and the institutional policies they should inquire about when weighing employment options. Doctoral students can also learn personal strategies for managing time and stress that may help them in the future. The academy will be stronger in the coming years if the new faculty are knowledgeable about options, policies, and strategies that help individuals create successful and productive careers and meaningful personal lives.

Concluding Comments

Today's academy is enriched by the inclusion of faculty members with diverse characteristics in terms of expertise, gender, race, age, family situation, and personal interests. Excellence should always be the hallmark of higher education institutions, and all faculty members should be held to the highest standards of quality in their work. But increasingly there is awareness that success does not mean all faculty members follow the same pattern in organizing their work. Many of today's faculty members are committed to finding ways to achieve excellence in their academic responsibilities while also fulfilling their responsibilities and interests as parents, family members, and citizens. If American universities and colleges are to attract and retain the array of faculty appropriate for a diverse society, we must acknowledge the multiple responsibilities that many faculty members manage. Attracting and retaining the best faculty will require institutional commitment to developing and implementing policies appropriate for diverse faculty circumstances. Institutional leaders and faculty members themselves will need to examine the culture and policies in place to ensure that all faculty members can fulfill their potential for professional excellence and their important personal responsibilities. This monograph explores issues concerning faculty roles and responsibilities and offers suggestions for strengthening the academic workplace so faculty can better manage professional and personal roles.

References

Austin, A. E. (2002, January/February). Preparing the next generation of faculty: Graduate education as socialization to the academic career. *Journal of Higher Education, 73*(2), 94–122.

Drago, R., & Williams, J. (2000). A half-time tenure track proposal. *Change, 32*(6), 46–51.

Nyquist, J. D., Manning, L., Wulff, D. H., Austin, A. E., Sprague, J., Fraser, P. K., et al. (1999, May/June). On the road to becoming a professor: The graduate student experience. *Change*, 18–27.

Rice, R. E., Sorcinelli, M. D., & Austin, A. E. (2000). *Heeding new voices: Academic careers for a new generation.* Washington, DC: American Association of Higher Education.

Additional Resources

Austin, A. E., & Gamson, Z. F. (1983). *The academic workplace: New demands, greater tensions.* ASHE-ERIC/Higher Education Research Report No. 10. Washington, D.C.: Association for the Study of Higher Education.

National Center for Education Statistics. (2001). *The integrated postsecondary education data system (IPEDS) salaries, tenure, and fringe benefits of full-time instructional faculty survey.* Washington, DC: Author.

National Center for Education Statistics. (2003). *The integrated postsecondary education data system (IPEDS) completions survey.* Washington, DC: Author.

Discussion and Focus Group Protocols and Demographic Surveys

Agencies of Change, University of Arizona

Dicussion Group Protocol

I.   Welcome, thank you for coming, introduction of facilitator and recorder

II.   Overview of the Project. This focus group is part of a larger multi-university project, funded by Rutgers University in association with the Ford Foundation and further supported by Southwest University, to better understand faculty initiatives for change. Specifically, the research team hopes to evaluate the impact of the faculty-led Faculty Climate Project, which was initiated by faculty leaders in 1999 to support development of an institutional culture at Southwest University that would foster productivity, creativity, and excellence among all faculty. In addition, we hope to examine the processes by which new structures continue to evolve in the university to bridge faculty and administrative roles in fostering institutional change and to understand what the successes and the barriers to success have been in instituting gender and racial/ethnic diversity at our institution.

To accomplish our goals, we are conducting a series of focus groups with faculty who have been involved in campus efforts related to the Faculty Climate Project. The information collected from each of these groups will be analyzed separately and held in the strictest confidence. Participation is strictly voluntary and individual names will be removed from the report and any related publications that result from this study.

III. Consent Forms. As a part of the university's human subjects policy, we need to have you read and sign a consent form. This form allows us to tape-record your views while assuring you that we will handle and process the information with the highest integrity in maintaining confidentiality.

IV.   Demographic Survey. Also, we would like you to take a moment to complete a demographic survey form that includes a few questions on how you currently view and experience the campus. Please DO NOT put your name on this form.

All consent forms will be kept separate from demographic survey data, in order to guarantee the anonymity of the demographic data. (Hand-out forms and pens/pencils; collect all forms before continuing.)

V.   Focus Group Ground Rules. As the facilitator, I will be leading you through a series of questions that focus on your experiences as a scholar, teacher, and colleague here at Southwest University. We would like you to answer honestly and articulate specific details that help us to understand your experience. It is quite likely that in your sharing you will reveal a range of emotions and feelings. We want to try to create a safe space for this to happen and so ask that each of you respect the others' perspectives and opinions. At times, you may disagree with something someone has said—we want to hear those disagreements and contrary positions, but would ask that you disagree with respect and civility. And please remember that anything said within this focus group is confidential. It would be inappropriate for you to share with others outside this group what you heard within the context of this focus group.

I would like to ask that you please speak up a little louder than normal when you address the group so that we can make sure that the tape recorder captures your voice. It would also be helpful if only one person speaks at a time since multiple, simultaneous voices make it difficult to hear and almost impossible to transcribe the flow of conversation from the tape.

VI.   Questions and Probes: (Begin tape recording)
1) What is the purpose of this organization?
2) What are the benefits of being involved in this (Faculty Climate Project) initiative?
3) What are the costs to being involved in this initiative?

4) How do you determine your agenda?
   a. What sorts of strategies do you and the organization use to advance your agenda?
   b. How do you engage others to help with the work?
5) How do you define success for this organization?
6) How is the initiative maintained?
   a. What steps are being taken to institutionalize the efforts of this organization?
7) Describe the level of administrative involvement.
   a. How would you like administrators to be involved?
8) What are some of the successes experienced as a result of the work of this organization?
9) What are some of the challenges you have faced in the work of this organization?
10) What environments encourage or discourage faculty participation?
11) What else would you like to share about the nature of your work in this organization that has not yet been covered?

VII. Is there anything else you would like to add or share that we haven't yet covered?

ABOUT THE EDITORS AND CONTRIBUTORS

Susan J. Bracken is an assistant professor of adult education at North Carolina State University in the department of adult and higher education. Her D.Ed. is from Pennsylvania State University, where she studied both adult education and women's studies. Her research interests include gender issues in adult and higher education, and adult learning in organizational contexts, particularly community engagement and community/university partnerships. She is currently the senior researcher on a National Science Foundation-funded research project that provides faculty instructional development to community college faculty in North Carolina and South Carolina. Before joining North Carolina State in 2004, she served as the special assistant to the vice president for outreach at Penn State University.

Jeanie K. Allen is a visiting assistant professor in interdisciplinary studies at Drury University in Springfield, Missouri. She holds a Ph.D. in higher education from Walden University, an M.Ed. from Drury University, a masters in accounting from the University of Arkansas, and a B.A. in zoology from the University of Arkansas. She currently teaches women's studies and interdisciplinary courses in American and global cultures. Her research interests include psychosocial development in women college students, organizational behavior in higher education, and adult learning in health care settings. Prior to her full-time faculty position, she served as director of academic advising and the First Year Experience Program at Drury University.

Diane R. Dean is assistant professor of higher education administration and policy at Illinois State University. Prior to her appointment, she was executive administrator for finance and administration at Teachers College, Columbia University. Dean holds an Ed.D. and M.A. in higher education administration from Columbia University and a B.A. in English and American literature from the University of Maryland, College Park. Her research and service interests center on the topics of higher education leadership, governance, policy, planning, diversity, and philosophical questions about the purpose and process of higher education.

Ann E. Austin is a professor at Michigan State University, holding the Mildred B. Erickson Distinguished Chair in higher, adult, and lifelong education. Her research concerns faculty careers and professional development, doctoral education, teaching and learning, and organizational change and transformation in higher education. She was a Fulbright Fellow in South Africa (1998), the 2001–2002 president of the Association for the Study of Higher Education (ASHE), and is currently co-principal investigator of the Center for the Integration of Research, Teaching, and Learning, a National Science Foundation Center focusing on the preparation of future faculty in Science, Technology, Engineering, and Mathematics (STEM) fields.

Mary Ann Mason is dean of the Graduate Division and a professor of social welfare and law at the University of California, Berkeley. Her Ph.D. in history is from the University of Rochester and her J.D. is from the University of San Francisco. She publishes and lectures nationally on child and family law matters and stepfamilies. Her current project is "Do Babies Matter? The Effects of Family Formation on the Careers of Academic Men and Women." She is co-principal investigator of the UC Faculty Family Friendly Edge Initiative. Her forthcoming book is titled *Mothers on the Fast Track: The Unfinished Revolution.*

Marc Goulden is a researcher at the University of California, Berkeley, studying work and family issues among faculty. He has a Ph.D. from the University of Wisconsin Madison (1995), with a focus on the diversity and life course of students in college and university settings. He works with Mary Ann Mason on the "Do Babies Matter" study and co-manages the UC Faculty Family Friendly Edge Initiative. These projects have resulted in articles and reports that have received considerable national attention. This last summer, the *Chronicle of Higher Education* profiled Goulden as one of "Higher Education's Next Generation of Thinkers."

Nicholas H. Wolfinger is associate professor in the Department of Family and Consumer Studies and adjunct associate professor of sociology at the University of Utah. He is the author of *Understanding the Divorce Cycle*

(Cambridge, MA: Cambridge University Press, 2005) and coeditor of *Fragile Families and the Marriage Agenda* (New York: Springer, 2005). His other projects include studying trends in the incomes of single mothers (with Matthew McKeever), the relationship between religion and well-being in urban America (with W. Bradford Wilcox), and the effects of family structure on voter turnout (with Raymond Wolfinger).

Carol L. Colbeck (Ph.D., Stanford University) is the director and a senior research associate in the Center for the Study of Higher Education, and associate professor of higher education at Pennsylvania State University. Colbeck's research investigates how social and organizational contexts shape academic work in four interrelated areas, (1) how faculty integrate teaching, research, and service; (2) how state, institutional, and departmental policies influence the nature and characteristics of faculty work; (3) how faculty teaching and organizational climate affect student learning; and (4) how faculty balance professional and personal responsibilities.

Elizabeth G. Creamer is an associate professor of educational research and evaluation at Virginia Tech and co-principal investigator of the Women and Information Technology project funded by the National Science Foundation, principal investigator of a grant to investigate climate in undergraduate engineering programs, and director of research and assessment for VTAdvance, another project funded by the National Science Foundation. Creamer's disciplinary background is in the field of higher education. Her research interests involve issues related to faculty careers, work, and lives, including gender differences in the factors associated with faculty publishing productivity. She is the author or coauthor of three books and forty-five refereed journal articles and scholarly book chapters.

Anna Neumann is professor of higher education at Teachers College, Columbia University; she was previously professor in educational psychology (studies of cognition and learning) at Michigan State University. Neumann studies scholarly learning across the life span with attention to college and university professors' intellectual development and doctoral students' learning of research. She is currently writing a book on professors' learning in early midcareer. Neumann's work has been published in the *Journal of Higher Education*, the *Review of Higher Education, American Educational Re-*

search Journal, Critical Inquiry, and *Journal of Aesthetic Education,* among others.

Aimee LaPointe Terosky received her doctorate in higher and postsecondary education with a specialization in teaching and learning from Teachers College, Columbia University. Her dissertation, *Taking Teaching Seriously: A Study of University Professors and Their Teaching,* was awarded the 2005 Bobby Wright Dissertation of the Year by the Association for the Study of Higher Education (ASHE). Currently, Terosky works as an educational technologist and researcher at Columbia University's Center for New Media Teaching and Learning (CCNMTL) and teaches in the higher and postsecondary education program at Teachers College as adjunct assistant professor.

Julie Schell is a doctoral student in higher and postsecondary education at Teachers College, Columbia University. Her areas of interest include faculty lives, diversity issues, scholarly inquiry, and college teaching and learning. She has a B.S. with distinction in health sciences and an M.S. in counseling and educational psychology from the University of Nevada, Reno. She is a recipient of a five-year fellowship from The Point Foundation.

Lisa Wolf-Wendel is an associate professor of higher education at the University of Kansas. She earned her doctorate in 1995 from the Claremont Graduate School and her bachelor's degree from Stanford University in 1987. Wolf-Wendel's research focuses on faculty issues, including a study of the academic labor market realities for faculty of color, and several research projects pertaining to the policy response of academic institutions in the wake of demands for dual-career couple accommodations. She recently published *The Two Body Problem: Dual Career Couple Hiring Practices in Higher Education* (Baltimore: Johns Hopkins University Press, 2003).

Kelly Ward is an associate professor of higher education at Washington State University. Her research is in the areas of junior faculty development, work and family issues for faculty, faculty involvement in student development, and campus and community relationships. Ward earned her Ph.D. in higher education from Pennsylvania State University. She is co-author of *Putting Students First: How Colleges Develop Students Purposefully* (Bolton, MA: Anker Publishing, 2006).

Jeni Hart is an assistant professor in the higher education and continuing education emphasis in the Department of Educational Leadership and Policy Analysis at the University of Missouri-Columbia. Hart has conducted research on activism among feminist faculty and the status and work lives of faculty women and faculty of color. In addition, she has coauthored two technical reports focused on campus climate issues for faculty and staff (emphasizing issues salient to women and people of color). Broadly, her agenda centers on gender issues, the professions, and organizational transformation within academe.

INDEX

fertility rate for, 15–16
at research universities, 51–52
Terosky, Aimee LaPointe, 6, 91, 94, 113, 116,
    120*n*, 150, 165
Theodore, A., 141
Thompson, R. J., 141
Tierney, W. G., 54, 91
time
    allocation by gender, 36, 39–40, 44–45
    correlation between personal and work, 33
    in developing agency, 115
time-based conflict, perception of, 33
Toutkoushian, R., 11
Trower, C. A., 74
Turner, C. S. V., 116, 141
two-body problem, 154
Twombly, S., 87

UC Faculty Family-Friendly Edge, 21
universities. *See* colleges and universities

Valian, Virginia, 11, 13, 133
Varner, A., 21
Vietnam War, 2

Wang, Y., 141, 143
Ward, Kelly, x–xi, 6, 52, 55, 56, 147–148, 150,
    151, 152, 155, 166
Watanabe, S., 33
Weick, K., 92
Weinstein, E. A., 74
*When Women ask the Questions: Women's
    Studies in America* (Boxer), 4
Williams, Joan, 3, 13, 20, 47, 151
Winslow, S. E., 32
Wolfinger, Nicholas H., 9, 12, 147, 148,
    164–165
Wolf-Wendel, Lisa, x–xi, 6, 52, 55, 56, 87,
    147–148, 150, 151, 152, 155, 166
women faculty. *See also* married women with
    children; tenure-track women
    degrees held by, 9
    dependent care responsibilities of, 32
    effects of family formation on tenure rates
        of, 11–15

in faculty, ix–x, 2, 9, 51, 147
impact of childbirth on, xi
as junior faculty, 72*n*, 148
satisfaction of, with time allocation, 44–45
service loads of academic, 116
social identities of, 2–3
tenure-track jobs for, x, 6, 12–13
work activities of, 39–40
women's movement, 2
women's studies, 1–8
    activism and, 5
    contemporary scholar-activists in, 5
    growth of, 4–5
    historical development of, 1–2, 3
    importance and contributions of, 1
    institution of higher education and, 2–5
    strategies for dealing with, 7–8
workaholism, 70
work boundaries, permeability of, 43
work environments
    creating positive and equitable, 7
    family-friendly, x–xi
work/family border theory, 35
work/family concerns, role of faculty union
        in addressing, 64–65
work/family conflict
    among University of California faculty
        parents, 19–20
    nature of, for academic parents, 9
    perceptions of, 32–33
    relationship of gender to, 36
work/family roles, satisfaction with, 32–33
work life, integration of, around a substan-
        tive focus, 96–101, 104–105
work/life policies, impact on faculty, 73
work roles, juggling of, by tenure-track fac-
        ulty, 31–48
work status, tenure track and, 16
work time, correlation between personal
        time and, 33
Wulff, D. H., xi, 155

Xie, Y, 11, 76, 87

Zuckerman, H., 11